SPENDING WAVES

HARRY S. DENT, JR.

SPENDING WAVES

*The Scientific Key To
Predicting Market Behavior
for the Next 20 Years*

HARRY S. DENT, JR.

2013

DENT RESEARCH

Dent Research
55 N.E. 5th Avenue, Suite 200
Delray Beach, FL 33483
Tel.: (561) 272-0413

ISBN 978-0-9789210-8-8

Copyright © 2013 Dent Research. All international and domestic rights reserved, protected by copyright laws of the United States and international treaties. No part of this publication may be reproduced in any form, printed or electronic or on the worldwide web, without written permission from the publisher, Dent Research, 55 N.E. 5th Avenue, Suite 200, Delray Beach, FL 33483.

Notice: This publication is designed to provide accurate and authoritative information in regard to the subject matter covered. It is sold and distributed with the understanding that the author, publisher and seller are not engaged in rendering legal, accounting or other professional advice or service. If legal or other expert assistance is required, the services of a competent professional advisor should be sought.

The information and recommendations contained herein have been compiled from sources considered reliable. Employees, officers and directors of Dent Research do not receive fees or commissions for any recommendations of services or products in this book. Investments and other recommendations carry inherent risks. As no investment recommendation can be guaranteed, Delray Publishing takes no responsibility for any loss or inconvenience if one chooses to accept them.

Table of Contents

Introduction 7

1. Education 31

2. House and Home 39

3. Sports and Recreation 57

4. Media 67

5. Furniture and Appliances 75

6. Home Goods 87

7. Home Services 107

8. Auto and Transportation 133

9. Children's Goods and Services 159

10. Clothing and Accessories for Adults 185

11. Computers and Electronics 207

12. Entertainment and Travel 213

13. Health Care 229

14. Professional Services 241

Conclusion 249

Notes 253

Introduction

In the rough and tumble world of business, we are conditioned not to think about things like "destiny." In America, you make your own luck, and those of us with the best ideas and the best execution, rise to the top. It is the American dream that good ideas and hard work are rewarded with material success.

This spirit is what makes the United States such a dynamic place, and it is what pushes the economy forward. It's what created modern world-dominating successes like Apple and Google, and the success stories of generations gone by, such as Ford and General Electric.

So long as America's entrepreneurs maintain that special spark, there will be no shortage of new opportunities in this country. It's important to keep this dream alive, and I'm not here to argue against it. But I am here to tell you that, in spite of my faith in American business, I do believe in destiny. And it's not always a charmed one.

You see, demography is destiny. It is the future that has already been written.[1] You just need to know how to read it.

Even politicians who are not always the sharpest people are able to instinctively grasp this concept. Did you notice the endless slicing and dicing of the American electorate both before and after last year's presidential election?

The media beat these statistics to death. Governor Romney carried the votes of white males over the age of 40, whereas President Obama performed better among women and among younger voters. But that's not where the number crunching stops. Not even close. These demographic groups can be broken down into subgroups and broken down again into even smaller sub-subgroups based on age, sex, marital status, income and more. I'm willing to bet you that strategists from both political parties could tell you the precise voting preferences of suburban-dwelling married Caucasian women with master's degrees, incomes in the 93rd percentile, exactly two children, and a strong preference for Coke over Pepsi. The information is out there and readily accessible; they would be fools not to use it.

Why does this kind of information matter? Because the success of any political candidate depends on his or her ability to know the preferences of the demographic groups that have the power to swing an election. Nixon had his Southern Strategy, George W. Bush captured America's suburbs, and Barack Obama took the votes of America's fastest-growing demographic groups. Republican or Democrat, whoever wins in 2016 will have done their demographic homework. I guarantee it.

Businesses, be they large multinationals or small mom-and-pop stores, also instinctively get demographics. If you hope to be successful, you have to know your market.

Think about it. The television commercials aired during Monday Night Football (think beer and macho pick-up trucks) are very different from the commercials aired during daytime soap operas (think baby products, food and diet-related products, and home exercise equipment). And both are different from the commercials aired during the Mickey Mouse Clubhouse or Dora the Explorer. With the dollar figures at stake, advertisers can't afford to waste resources targeting the wrong viewership.

Similarly, at the small business level, you don't open a store that sells baby strollers next to a college campus or open a trendy bar in a retirement community. The local convenience store owner knows whether he should be stocking baby diapers or adult diapers. (Incidentally, Japan started selling more adult diapers than baby diapers in 2011.[2] They've also started making shopping carts at grocery stores lighter weight so that an older person can push them more easily.

The key is that you know who your customers are. You have to, or you won't be in business for long. The majority of small businesses fail within five years of their founding. The most cited reason is a lack of investment capital, but the real reason is often a lot simpler: Many businesses fail due to a misunderstanding of their target market.

But even if you do understand your core market, that may not be enough. It's an important first step, but even if you understand your market perfectly well, you can still see your business swept away by an unstoppable wave of changing demographics.

Just ask Harley-Davidson about shifting demographics.

Harley-Davidson knows its core market. The stereotypical riders of its iconic chrome-laden motorcycles are almost exclusively white men in their mid-to-late 40s—the classic age for a man to have a mid-life crisis, grow a beard, and wear a dew rag. And the data confirms this: Spending on large motorcycles peaks between the ages of 45 and 49.

Harley-Davidson had a fantastic run supplying its hogs to Baby Boomer men as they went through this stage of their lives. But then, suddenly, it all came crashing to a halt. Harley has had a terrible time growing its sales in the post-2008 economy and not just because unemployment is high or credit is tight. As Alex Taylor wrote in the September 17, 2010 edition of *Fortune*, Harley-Davidson is "struggling against a foe that not even cost-cutting or brand loyalty can overcome: demographics. Its current owners are getting old, and not enough younger ones are coming up behind them."[3]

We'll get into the specifics of how to track demographic trends shortly. But the key point for you to take away here is that changes are coming—major changes that will affect your business in ways you have probably never considered.

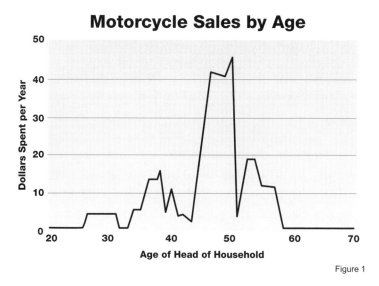

Figure 1

It is my job to show you what is coming so that you know how best to prepare. After reading this book, you may decide to make major changes to your business. You may decide to expand… or to hold off on expansion. In the most extreme cases, you may decide that it makes sense to close up shop and start something new. I'm going to give you the tools you need to make that decision.

What Really Drives the Economy

As you read along, you are probably nodding your head in understanding. Ordinary Americans instinctively understand demographics and they see how it affects their lives, their businesses and the economy as a whole.

Yet, with very few exceptions, economists and most investment professionals are still clueless about demographics. I've made the comment in presentations that sex ultimately drives the economy, and it usually gets a few nervous laughs from the room. But it is a completely accurate statement. The family life cycle drives our consumer spending, and it all starts with sex.

That economists don't grasp this concept is due to either remarkably closed minds or to their lack of a sex life. I'll let you draw your own conclusions as to which it might be.

To understand what I'm talking about, think about your own life and family. We all like to think that we are unique and special, but when it comes to our basic consumer behavior by age and stage of life, we are remarkably predictable. Let's start with the birth of a child.

For starters, it's going to be expensive. The cost to raise a child from birth to age 17 is $368,000 for an urban, educated couple, according to U.S. government estimates. The figure for lower income families is smaller but not nearly as small as you might think. For the lowest-income groups (defined here as a family with an average income of $38,000), the figure is still a mind-blowing $150,000 per child.

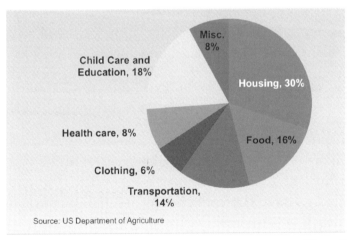

Figure 2

The real figure across all income groups is much higher than these estimates because few 17-year-olds are financially independent. It's not uncommon for parents to at least partially support their kids well into their 20s, and we've said nothing about the cost of a college education. You can tack on another $100,000 to $200,000 per child for that... and maybe more if you offer to pay for their graduate school. And if they opt for medical school, you have my condolences. You're talking about million-dollar babies at that point.

Where does all the money go? The biggest increases in expenditures are due to lifestyle changes. You need a bigger home... and preferably one with a yard. Housing accounts for 30% of child-related expenses. You have new mouths to feed, quite literally. Food adds another 16%. You probably need a bigger car... or a gas-guzzling SUV. And you probably now have a longer commute and more errands that need to be run. Transportation adds another 14%. Clothes? Throw in 6% more.

Given the sky-high cost of health insurance these days, it's surprising that health care spending is only 8% of the pie, though for most Americans the bulk of health care costs are paid for by employer-sponsored health insurance. This is changing, as high costs are forcing companies to be less generous, and Americans will be spending more on their families' health care going forward.

After housing, food and health care, child care and non-university education take up most of the rest, at 18%.

This doesn't tell the whole story, of course. The government figures also don't take into account the harder-to-measure cost factors, such as being "mommy tracked" or passed over for promotions due to family obligations. This could be worth hundreds of thousands of dollars in lost wages, or perhaps even millions if your skills are in high demand or if you have an advanced degree.

By *The New York Times* estimates, the cost to raise kids is closer to $700,000 per child and, again, this doesn't include college.[4] It also doesn't include socialized costs such as the taxes you pay for public schools.

If you have three children, it will cost you more than $2 million to raise them, and maybe another half a million or more to educate them. That's daunting to even think about. You might want to drop this book and get back to work—you have very expensive mouths to feed!

I go into this level of excruciating detail for a reason. If you are a parent, what I am saying will seem very real to you because you're the one paying these bills. This isn't abstract theory; it's real life. And it's important to understand for the sections to come.

When a baby is conceived, we already know with high probability how his or her life will unfold (Figures 3–6). The pregnancy and birth will be expensive to the parents but will be a boon to everything from pediatrician offices to baby clothes makers to early childhood development classes.

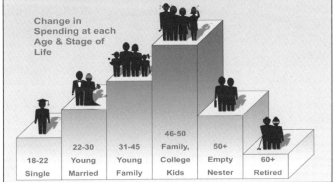

Figure 3

The child will start school at age five and presumably graduate by age 18, after which most Americans go on to some level of higher education. If a boy, he will probably get married around the age of 28. If a girl, it will be closer to 26. And they will have children of their own shortly thereafter.

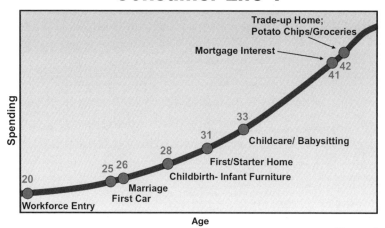

Figure 4

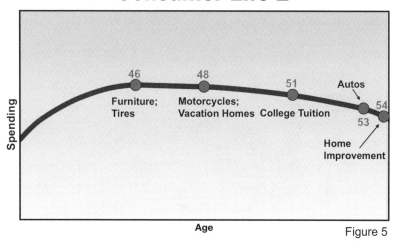

Figure 5

The ages for first marriage and childbirth tend to be a little older the higher up the income and education ladder you go. Again, this makes sense. The longer you stay in higher education, the longer you postpone family formation. Everything gets pushed back by a few years. As such, Americans with lower levels of formal education and lower incomes have children around 27, with higher-educated and higher-income Americans having kids at close to 29.

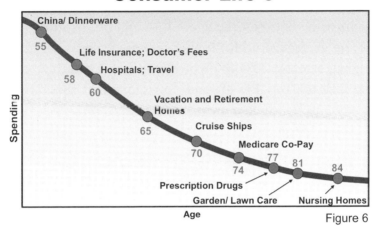

Figure 6

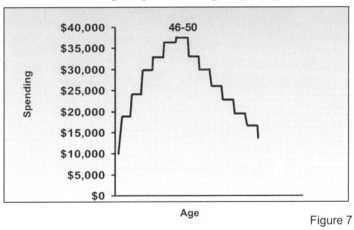

Figure 7

With children, come the need for houses. Starter-home purchases peak around age 31, and for those Americans who upgrade, trade-up home purchases peak around age 42. We'll jump into real estate in more detail in Chapter 2, but I include this data here to make an important point. A home is the most expensive asset most American families will ever own, and home spending is driven almost entirely by demographics.

As for consumer spending (Figure 7), it rises every year of your life until your kids finally leave the nest. For most Americans, this will happen sometime between the ages of 45 and 50, or more precisely at age 46, on average. And for higher-income Americans, that age is a little higher. The top 10% of income earners peak in their spending at 50–51, and the top 1% around 53. Remember this range—it's going to come in handy in a minute.

As we get into our 50s, we start to spend less and save more. Retirement is still years away, but with the kids out of the house, we're finally in a better position to sock money away. So, even while we work harder and earn more than at any other stage of our lives, we're spending less. And once we get into our late 60s and 70s, our spending falls even further. Frankly, at that stage of our lives, we already own everything we want, and most of us are living in retirement on a fixed income. We may still live to be 100, but by our 60s we've already reached the last stage of the consumer life cycle.

By the way, you don't have to take my word for it on any of this. My data comes directly from the U.S. government. The Bureau of Labor Statistics Consumer Expenditure Survey[5] annually tracks the spending habits of American consumers and breaks them down by age, sex, income level and so on. This is where I got the data for motorcycles and for total consumer spending and it's going to be the focus for most of the rest of this book. I'm going to break down the U.S. retail economy and detail the products and services that demographic trends suggest should boom… and those that demographic trends suggest should bust.

But before I do that, I want to step back and take a look at the broader picture. No matter how good or bad the demographic trends might be, the overall health of the economy matters. And yes, demographics play a major role here as well.

The Great Boom and the Great Bust

You've heard the expression "a rising tide lifts all boats," and nowhere is this more true than in the case of demographics and the economy. The great boom of the 1980s, 1990s and mid-2000s was due to the maturing of the largest and wealthiest generation in history, the Baby Boomers. And the stagnant economy we've endured for the past five years is largely the result of those same Baby Boomers reaching a different stage of their lives. Remember my comment about Americans reaching their peak spending years between the ages of 45 and 50? You're about to see why that matters.

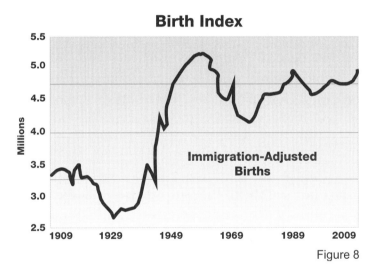

Figure 8

Take a look at Figure 8, the Immigration-Adjusted Birth Index, one of the main building blocks of HS Dent research. There is no rocket science here; this graph is nothing more than the annual live births in the United States adjusted for immigration. Immigrants are added to the index in the year they were born in their respective home country. So, a 30-year-old immigrant who comes to the United States in 2013 shows up as a birth in 1983.

You notice the enormous bulge in the middle of the graph? That's the Baby Boomer generation, the proverbial pig passing through a python.

Though ridiculed by some as the "Me Generation," the Baby Boomers might be forgiven for believing the world revolves around them because for much of the past 50 years, the economic world really has revolved around them. By their sheer size, they have been a major disruptive force in the economy since their birth, and they are a major focus of HS Dent research.

This generation—perhaps more than any other in history — has truly defined our age. Their births in the years following World War II brought us the massive expansion of the American suburbs, as their parents needed bigger homes in which to raise them. The surge in the number of school-aged children necessitated school construction on a massive, unprecedented scale. As they become teenagers and young adults, the rock & roll culture they created led to a cultural and social revolution.

In the 1970s, the largest generation in history began to enter the workforce en masse. Not shockingly, the entry of millions of young, untrained workers led to the biggest eruption of peacetime inflation in American history. As Boomer workers gained experience in the 1980s, productivity surged, inflation fell, and the economy reached new highs. The 1980s "Decade of Greed" was largely a result of the Boomers getting haircuts and real jobs, rolling up their sleeves, and getting to work. Similarly, the technology revolution of the 1990s was the result of the innovations of Boomers like Steve Jobs and Bill Gates that went mainstream, leveraged by the disruptive power of the Internet.

Stop reading for a minute and think back to the early 1990s. With the benefit of 20 years of hindsight, it seems obvious that a major boom was inevitable. And indeed, I was saying as much—my 1992 book was titled *The Great Boom Ahead*.

But it sure didn't seem that way to most people at the time. American industry was in decline… and getting routed by nimbler Japanese competitors. Our budget deficits were sky high. We were just coming out of a nasty recession. Unemployment was high. And of course, there was that now infamous "sucking sound" of American jobs going to Mexico that presidential candidate Ross Perot warned of.

In spite of the "obvious" evidence of gloom, I knew without a doubt that a major boom was about to get underway. And I knew it from looking at Figure 9: The Spending Wave.

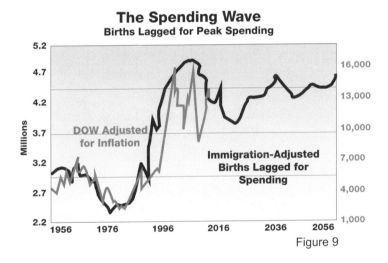

Figure 9

The Spending Wave takes the Immigration-Adjusted Birth Index and adds our insights about peak spending by age. If we know that average Americans peak in their spending at age 46, we can turn the birth year into a forecasting model for consumer spending.

And how do the numbers play out? Let's take a look. The baby boom peak was 1961. This means that the biggest cohort of the Baby Boomers would be hitting their peak spending years 46 years later in 2007, which just happened to correspond with the end of a multi-decade boom.

To be clear, this kind of demographic analysis is a broad sword, not a surgical scalpel. In the real economy, there are forces that can cause a demographic forecast to be off by a year or two. Government spending, strong exports and foreign trade, strong business investment, and a loose banking system can all keep an economy booming in the short term, and a lack of any of these can depress an economy in the short term. But there is no escaping the broader macro trend. Over any real timeline, demographics will trump everything else, even the almighty Federal Reserve and U.S. government.

As early as 1992, I forecasted that the boom of the 1990s and 2000s would turn into a nasty bust by 2008, and this proved to be accurate. As if on cue, the Baby Boomers have reduced their spending and started saving more.

How much more? During the boom years of the 2000s, it fell to as low as 0.9%. Americans saved less than 1% of their incomes. But by the middle of 2008, it had soared to over 8%, and it has remained relatively high ever since.

This is good for the Boomers, of course, but it's bad for the rest of us. More than 70 years ago, noted economist John Maynard Keynes wrote about the paradox of thrift,[6] in which what it good for the individual saver—to frugally save money—is bad for the economy as a whole. If everyone saves at the same time, then economic activity grinds to a halt. The economy goes into bunker mode.

That is our situation today, and it's not getting better any time soon.

The Big Picture: A Rough Economy until the 2020s

Ever since the financial meltdown of 2008 it's been rough out there. The year 2008 is what I call the "Great Reset," when our economy was knocked out of high growth mode (Figure 10). We returned to growth in 2010, but we never made it back to the old trend. Not even close. Growth has been slow and uneven, and the crisis left a massive gap of lost growth that we will never get back. This is precisely what I was talking about in my 2008 book *The Great Depression Ahead*.

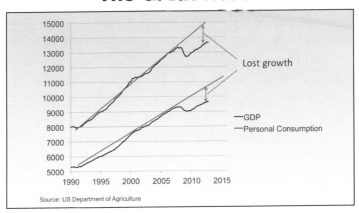

Figure 10

There is one big piece of all of this that I have left out. Demographic trends are slow-moving, whereas the collapse in 2008 was swift and violent. What's the connection?

The key here is leverage. During the boom years, the availability of cheap credit is like gasoline on a fire. In high enough doses, it can turn a flickering flame into a raging inferno.

Debt makes it possible to purchase things today that would normally have been purchased at some point in the future. Debt is a facilitator that turns latent demand into real consumption. So, it makes the booms much, much bigger than they would have been.

The flip side of this is that it makes the bust much, much worse. In our present case, not only have the Baby Boomers naturally slowed their spending due to the consumer life cycle, they are also paying down the debts from the three-decade boom.

And it's not just the Boomers themselves; it's the entire financial system that sprung up to meet their needs. The good news is that the deleveraging process is already well on its way. But the bad news is that it still has a long way to go. Take a look at Figure 11. You can see that financial sector debt exploded after 1990, completely dwarfing all other types of debt. Mortgages also exploded starting around the year 2000 as the loose credit standards that fueled the housing boom were just getting underway. These are now the two sectors shrinking the fastest, and that's not going to change any time this decade. The financial sector simply got too big during the boom, and you can't "right size" something that big overnight. It takes time.

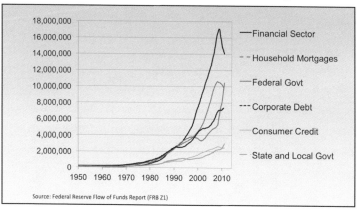

Figure 11

The deleveraging of the U.S. economy will ultimately make it stronger and more robust. But it's not going to be fun getting to that point. A dollar used to pay off debt is a dollar not spent in the economy. And if you're a business owner, it's a dollar not collected in your cash register.

Deleveraging goes hand in hand with deflation, or falling prices, because deleveraging reduces consumer demand and destroys dollars that were created by excessive debt in the bubble. When supply is as strong as ever but demand is weak, you end up with overcapacity. And overcapacity means falling prices. Just think of your local car lot. What does the sales manager do when he has a lot full of unsold cars? He lowers the price.

Deflation: It's Happened Before

It's hard to run a business in a deflationary environment. Your customers have little urgency to buy—and even less incentive to buy on credit—because they know that prices will be lower if they just wait awhile. Once deflation sets in, it can be something of a self-fulfilling prophecy. Prices fall because we expect them to fall. And this works its way all the way up the supply chain. If the retailer has to lower its prices, then so do its suppliers. It's an absolute nightmare for anyone running a business.

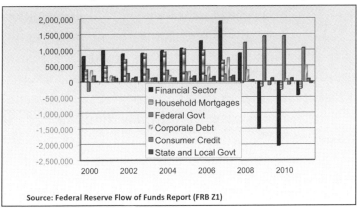

Figure 12

The last time the United States had significant deflation was during the Great Depression of the 1930s. There is, however, a more recent example on the other side of the Pacific and one that is more relevant to our situation today.

I'm talking about Japan. Japan went through a debt bubble and crisis two decades ago that was very similar to ours, and it provides a sobering vision of our future.

Japan was the first emerging market "miracle" economy in the years following World War II. No country in history could match Japan's growth rates from the 1950s through the 1970s. In just three decades, Japan evolved from a shelled-out warzone into an industrial powerhouse that rivaled the United States.

By the 1980s, Americans suddenly found themselves struggling to compete with Japanese manufacturers of steel, autos and consumer electronics. The world clamored to learn Japanese. Everywhere, Japan Inc. was on the offensive. Remember the future portrayed in the 1989 movie *Back to the Future Part II*? Michael J. Fox's character gets to see what his life will be like in 2015, and his boss is Japanese, calling from Tokyo.

The Japanese stock market had a wild ride. Between 1985 and 1990 the Nikkei tripled, hitting a high just shy of 40,000 in December of 1989. Not to be outdone, the Japanese real estate bubble made the stock market bubble look like child's play. Just as we saw in Florida, California, and other bubble markets in the mid-2000s, home prices in Tokyo far outpaced incomes and reached highs that would have seemed absurd in more sober times. Hundred-year multigenerational mortgages became a necessity in order to afford a modest apartment in Tokyo. At its peak, Japanese property was worth four times that of the entire United States, and the area around the Imperial Palace alone was gauged to be more valuable than the state of California—Silicon Valley and all.

Those bubble days are long gone, and today we see a very different Japan. Japanese stocks and urban land values are still down 75% and 70% respectively from their peaks two decades ago. Japan has spent the last 20 years in and out of recession, unable to gain any real momentum. It's the modern-day equivalent of a depression… except it never ended and still persists to this day. It's actually more like a "coma" economy due to endless money printing to ease the pain, but that doesn't allow debt to deleverage for longer-term health.

Japan's Collapse was Predictable

The collapse of Japan took everyone from expert economists to Wall Street establishments by surprise. But it would have been easy to predict if they had simply known where to look. And by the way, I did know where to look, and I successfully forecasted Japan's implosion in my first book *Our Power to Predict* (1989) and in its follow-up, *The Great Boom Ahead* (1993).

Japan did not have a post-war baby boom on the scale of America's. So Japan's Spending Wave peaked long before ours, in 1989 (Japanese spending peaks around age 47). And what followed in Japan is exactly what you should expect in an overleveraged economy that depended heavily on one large generation that had already peaked in spending. The situation was made more extreme by an over-leveraged, over-indebted population, corporate sector, and banking sector, but Japan's slow-motion depression would have happened in any event. The demographic story had already been written.

But surely it can't get that bad here. What about Bernanke's quantitative easing? And what about all of that government stimulus we've been paying for? Surely trillion-dollar deficits count for something, right?

As the Japanese crisis wore on, the Bank of Japan cut interest rates from 6% to zero, giving money away in the hopes that someone would spend it. Sound familiar? In the standard formula, lowering interest rates is supposed to boost consumption and investment.

But it didn't quite work out like that. Interest rates dropped, but savings remained high. Consumer spending stayed flat and then fell. New investment in productive assets stalled; Japanese businesses already had more than enough capacity. Japan did not stop with central bank monetary policy. The government launched countless fiscal stimulus programs, most of which caused a brief blip in growth but led to no lasting effect. The once fiscally conservative Japanese government went on the largest public works spending spree in history, boosting its budget deficits and government debts to levels rarely seen in developed countries.

Today, Japan has 30 times the amount of land covered in concrete as the United States, adjusting for the size difference in the two countries, and over 2,800 river dams. But none of this was enough to jolt an economy dragged down by deleveraging and bad demographics. It didn't work for Japan, and it won't work for the United States either.

I've rambled on about Japan long enough for you to get my point. This demographic forecasting isn't theoretical. It is real, very real, and we see it coming to life in the world around us. My forecast was correct in Japan, and it has been correct here so far.

Twenty years after the bubble burst, Japan is still struggling with deflation. We won't have 20 years of deflation here; I expect us to return to "normal" inflation by early next decade. But that is still a decade away, and in the meantime we still have to operate in a rough economy.

So, how do we operate in a deflationary environment?

As I wrote in *The Great Crash Ahead*, deflation is not an equal-opportunity destroyer. It comes once in a lifetime in the longer-term business cycle, and it determines which businesses are going to survive and which businesses are going to fail. It shakes out the weak and the unprepared, but it also makes room for the stronger competitors to grow and gain market share. My goal is to make you one of those survivors.

In *The Great Crash Ahead*, I laid out a general blueprint for surviving a long deflationary shakeout:

- Position your business so that you are not overly dependent on credit from a deleveraging financial system.

- Focus on the core areas of your business that you dominate today and that you can realistically expect to dominate in the future.

- Shed assets and business segments where you are weaker or where you have a harder time differentiating yourself from the competition.

- Make only short-term investments in marketing and promotional efforts that can grow your business or in investments that can help you cut costs.

- Defer major capital investments until later in the decade, when you will likely be able to buy them more cheaply.

And to this list I would add one final addition. If your business is particularly at risk to a decline in your core customer demographic, consider radically changing the direction of your company or starting a new business altogether. The next 7–10 years will be some of the most challenging in your career, but the foundations you lay today will put you in position to prosper in the global boom ahead.

Surfing the Spending Waves

In the sections that follow, we'll take a look at the demographic buying patterns of over 200 common consumer products with the idea of applying these insights to your business and to your family's decision making.

First, a little background on the data is in order. All of the data used came directly from the U.S. Government's Consumer Expenditure Survey (CES). The CES consists of two separate surveys, the Quarterly Interview Survey and the Diary Survey. The Diary tracks expenditures over the preceding two weeks. So, given that some of the data is quarterly and some is biweekly, a little cleanup is needed to make the data usable.

First, we combined the data for the past decade to get a larger sample size. Then, we tested for statistical significance to eliminate any products for which the data was too thin to use or inconclusive. Next, in order to eliminate the statistical noise, we added a polynomial trend line to smooth out the graphs. And finally, in order to make sense of the dollar amounts, we indexed all amounts to the spending level of a 20-year-old. So, for example, if a 50-year-old consumer has a value of 2.5 on the bedroom linens chart, that means that a 50-year-old consumer spends two and a half times as much on sheets and pillow cases as a 20-year-old.

The final result is a series of graphs that I can confidently say are both accurate and easy to understand.

There is one final idiosyncrasy that I should mention to avoid any confusion. For the math majors out there, we used a six-factor polynomial for the trend line because it gave us the truest match to the raw data. But the one drawback to this kind of trend line is that the far tails can get a little skewed, particularly if the data is thin. For example, in the graph for Furniture Repair, Refurnishing or Reupholstery, you will see a huge spike after the age of 80. That is something you can safely ignore. Throughout the text, I'll try to note the graphs that have this issue, but you can follow a general rule of thumb: If you see abnormally large spikes with no apparent explanation, it's probably a case of the trend line overcompensating. You can safely ignore the tails in these cases.

How Do I Use This Book?

Think back to the section above where I laid out the rationale for the Immigration-Adjusted Birth Index and the Spending Wave. In order for a product or service to profit from the aging of the Baby Boomers, it needs to have a peak age of late 50s or older. Remember, the largest cohort of the Baby Boomers has already passed the age of 50. So unless a product appeals to a consumer close to the age of 60 or (preferably) later, you've already missed the Boomer wave.

The next great generation is Generation Y, also known as the Echo Boomers or the Millennial generation. The largest cohort of this generation just passed the age of 20, so products with a peak demand age of late 20s to early 40s have an excellent demographic forecast in front of them.

These are really your two best avenues for growth. You either orient your business to sell to the wave or aging Boomers or you orient your business to sell to their children, who are starting their careers and the family formation cycle. And if your product or service is a "tweener" that appeals to an age group other than the Boomers or the Echo Boomers, you might have some difficult choices to make in the very near future.

Without further ado, let's jump into the data.

This page intentionally left blank.

Education

EDUCATION

We'll start with an expense area that may be more useful in your personal life than in your business life unless your business happens to concern education. But if you invest or are considering investing in property—such as rental housing for students or recent graduates—this section is one you won't want to miss.

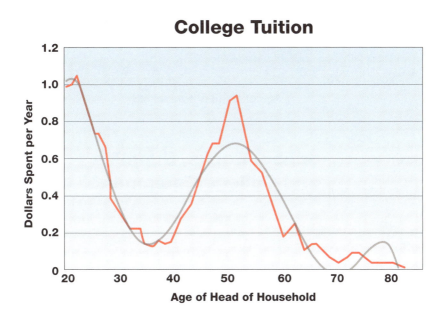

Figure 1.1

Figure 1.1 tracks college tuition, and there are no surprises here. There are three distinct peaks corresponding to the college kids themselves into their early 20s, to their parents around the age of 50–51 and to their grandparents in to age 73–74. The results here are intuitive and exactly what you would expect to see. Figure 1.2 tells the exact same story and has peaks at the very similar ages.

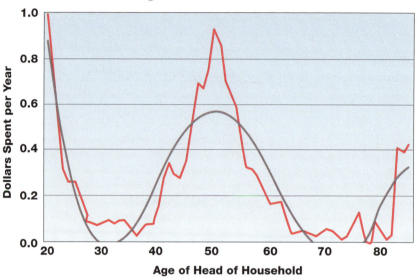

Figure 1.2

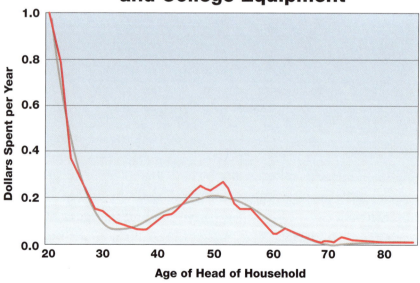

Figure 1.3

With college books and supplies (Figure 1.3), there is less help from parents and grandparents, though this is probably due more to the way the survey questions are phrased than to any fundamental difference in spending patterns. Students do the actual buying in the bookstore, though it is often with their parents' money.

Based on the Immigration-Adjusted Birth Index, we have lean times coming. This may come as a surprise to you if you've been following the news or if you have children that are at or near college age. There has been talk of a "college tuition bubble" and with good reason. In 2012, the total balance of student loans outstanding rose higher than credit card debt for the first time in history.[7] And last year college seniors graduated with the highest debt levels in history with an average of nearly $27,000,[8] though debts of well over $100,000 are not uncommon for students with graduate degrees or even undergraduate degrees at the most prestigious schools.

It's no wonder when you consider that the cost of a college degree has risen by nearly 1,200% since 1978 — double the rate of inflation for health care, another area where costs have spiraled out of control.[9]

One reason for the explosion in the price of a college education is the increased importance of having one. Wages for skilled professionals have massively outpaced wages for non-skilled labor over the past two decades, and the unemployment rate gets significantly lower the higher up the educational food chain you go.

By Bureau of Labor Statistics (BLS) estimates, the unemployment rate for all American workers was 7.9% as of January 2013.[10] But for those with only a high school diploma or for those who hadn't finished high school, the rate shot up to 8.3% and 12.4%, respectively. Unemployment for those with college degrees was 3.8%. For workers with a master's degree, the unemployment rate was only 3.5%, and for those with professional degrees (i.e. medicine, law, etc.) the number fell to just 2.1%.

Oh, and weekly earnings of those with even a basic bachelor's degree were double those of workers who never finished high school and 40% higher than those with a high school diploma.

Money talks. And for all the headlines you see about delinquency and low educational attainment in the United States, a record number of young Americans have earned a bachelor's degree. In fact, 33% of all 25-to-29-year-olds have a bachelor's degree, and fully 63% have completed some amount of college. That is nearly double the rate of the 1970s.[11]

This is yet another reason why I am optimistic about the future. The young people of today will be the innovators that lead the next great technology boom of the 2020s.

That said, the proportion of young people going to college has leveled off in recent years and probably doesn't have much further to rise. Much of the rise in the percentage of Americans going to higher education since the 1970s consisted of women "catching up" to men, and that process was completed long ago. In fact, young women are now significantly better educated than young men. So, education is becoming even more dependent on age demographic trends than ever before. And the demographics aren't good for the next few years.

The peak in Echo Boomers turning 18 — the year that most start college — peaked in 2008 and started a seven-year decline. The number of 18-year-olds coming down the pipeline starts to pick up again in 2015 and continues well into the 2020s. So, if you do intend to launch or expand a business that caters to a college clientele (think everything from bars to smoothie shops in college towns) or if you intend to invest in student housing, the time to do it would be within the next 2–3 years. You shouldn't overpay, of course, but if you can find an opportunity to buy from a developer or business owner who overextended themselves during the boom and is willing to cut a deal, then you should by all means take advantage of the opportunity.

Just make sure that the cash flow will be sufficient for the next few years before the boom really gets underway again.

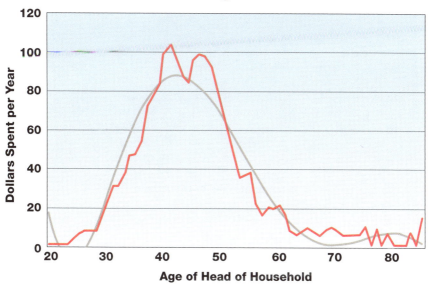

Figure 1.4

Moving on, we have very different spending patterns for elementary and high school tuition than we do for university education. Grandparents contribute relatively little, and the students themselves obviously contribute nothing. Private school is purely the responsibility of the moms and dads who can afford it.

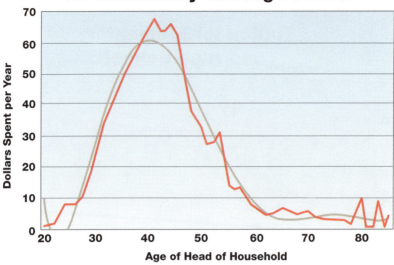

Figure 1.5

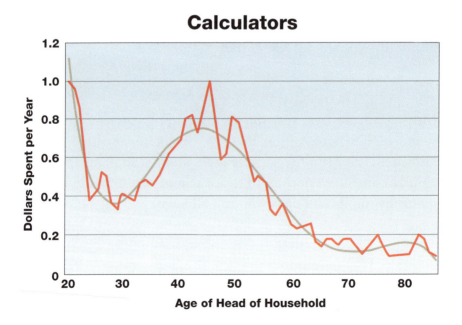

Figure 1.6

Spending on private tuition peaks at age 41 and stays very high into the late 40s, which makes sense. Spending on books and supplies peaks at exactly the same time. Spending on calculators (Figure 1.6) peaks at college age but has a secondary peak at age 42, in line with books and supplies.

Again, these figures make sense. If you have a child in your mid-20s to early 30s, that child will be 10–15 years old by the time you are 40. And you may be paying tuition for more than one child!

This is a less-investable theme than the college wave. Few entrepreneurs are going to start a new private school. And even if you did, it would be years or decades before your school was competitive on a reputational level.

Still, there are opportunities for school-related expenses, particularly sporting equipment, musical instruments and other expensive extracurricular activities. I'll get to those in a later section.

There are some figures to keep in mind for all child-related products and services. The number of live births reached a peak in 1990 before going into a 7-year decline. Births then hit a new all-time high in 2007 at 4,316,233 before falling sharply due to the financial crisis. (But note that adjusted for immigration, total birth rates for the Echo Boomers never got as high as the peak of the Baby Boomers.) Couples who thought about starting a family or having another child thought twice about it after their home values collapsed and seeing the economy screech to a halt.

The U.S. birth rate actually hit an all-time low in 2011, according to the Centers for Disease Control and Prevention (CDC),[12] at 63.2 births per 1000 women of child-bearing age. But the rate is very different from the raw number. In 2011, there were 3,953,593 babies born, which was a good 1% lower than 2010 and about 8.5% lower than the 2007 peak. The decline in the raw number is less pronounced than the decline in the birth rate due to a large increase in the number of women of childbearing age. In other words, mothers are having fewer kids… but there are still a massive number of mothers out there.

In a nutshell, women are having fewer babies due to the bad economy and that is likely to continue into the early 2020s. At the same time, the first wave of Echo Boomers that peaked in 1990 will be reaching their prime childbearing ages. Without the bad economy, we would likely be seeing a mini baby boom right now, but births are likely to be flat into the early 2020s and then somewhat flat in the early stages of the next boom until the second wave of Echo Boomers hits its prime childbearing age during a good economy from 2027 to 2036.

For entrepreneurs, this is a great opportunity, and I have another section dedicated to it. But the key takeaway from this chapter is that the wave of babies that crested in 2007 means there is a wave of 5-year olds this year in 2013… and thus a wave of 18-year olds coming in 2025. This means big demand for primary and secondary education for years to come and for all of the industries that support education.

House and Home

HOUSE AND HOME

There is no sector of the economy more controversial today than housing. Housing gave us the last great investment bubble—and made millionaires out of plenty of nimble speculators—but when the subprime market started to crumble in 2008, it set into motion a chain of events that forever tarnished homeownership in the minds of millions of Americans.

This is really a pity because housing is one of the sectors most driven by demographic trends and thus easiest to understand and forecast. At the right price and under the right conditions, housing is a fantastic investment that takes advantage of easy-money leverage. And due to high non-cash depreciation charges, it is often possible to generate a nice stream of current income while paying little or no income tax. And if you take advantage of certain aspects of the tax code, such as a 1031 exchange, you can avoid paying capital gains taxes as well. There are few investments out there that legally offer these kinds of advantages.

But notice that I said that real estate is a fantastic investment "under the right conditions." Under the wrong conditions, it is a highly leveraged investment nightmare with the potential to ruin you financially.

So, what are the right conditions? To start, you want inflation and, ideally, a low interest rate. We definitely have the low interest rate environment today. Borrowers with good credit can get a standard 30-year fixed-rate mortgage for well under 4%. But what about the inflation?

As you read in the introduction, I believe that deflation will continue to wreak havoc on our economy and financial system off and on for the rest of this decade. The Baby Boomers—the largest and richest generation in history—are paying down their debt load as they prepare for retirement, and by doing so they are sucking liquidity and purchasing power out of the economy.

But it's not just the Boomers. The banking system that sprung up to meet their needs is shrinking as well, due to both government regulation and their own belated realization that high leverage is risky.

Why does this matter? Look at figure 2.1. Over time, housing prices have tracked the rate of inflation. As you can see in the graph, the housing bubble of the 2000s was a major anomaly that jumps off the line like a spike.

Most of the returns that investors and homeowners have enjoyed from owning a home are due to inflation and leverage. A typical down payment on a primary residence is 5–10% (though it is usually significantly higher on investment properties). After a very modest initial investment, you pay back the loan over 30 years in dollars that are continually depreciated by inflation. It all works splendidly…except when there is no inflation.

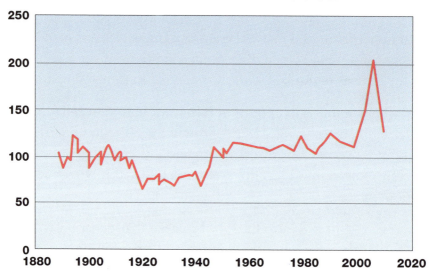

Figure 2.1

In a deflationary environment, all of this goes in reverse. You pay back your loan in dollars that get increasingly more valuable with each passing year, even while the market value of the house continues to sag. If you owned a home in one of the states hit hardest during the property crash, such as Florida, California, Arizona or Nevada, you know exactly what I'm talking about.

So, in an environment of broad-based deflation, we have to be careful how we invest. But this doesn't mean that there will not be great opportunities in real estate for those who are patient and know where to look.

There is an old expression that the three rules that every real estate buyer should consider are "location, location and location." I won't argue with this colloquial wisdom, but I will add to it. Location should not just be thought of as neighborhood or a prestigious zip code. Instead, think of location as where demographic trends are driving people. This is the single most important rule of real estate investment and ultimately the only one that matters. Strong demographic trends can create inflation in certain areas of the market even in an environment of broad-based deflation. But you have to make sure that you are on the right side of this. It will make the difference between profitable investment and financial ruin.

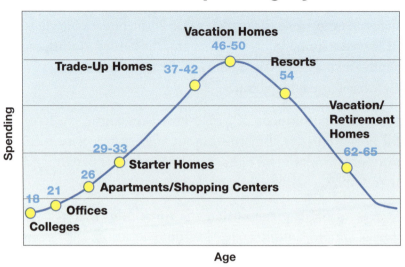

Figure 2.2

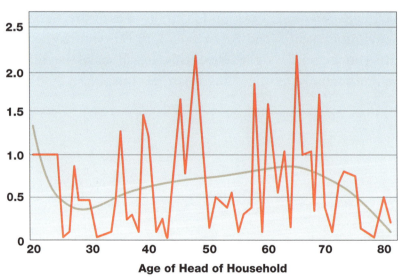

Figure 2.3

So where are the demographic trends heading? Take a look at Figure 2.2. The basic real estate life cycle is easy enough to understand. When we turn 18, we drive demand for college housing and low-rent apartments. In our early 20s, after we graduate and start our careers, we drive demand for office space, for apartments, and for the retail and entertainment properties that service both. After we get married and start families in our late 20s or early 30s, we drive demand for starter homes. And many of us go on to buy trade-up "McMansion" homes in our late 30s and early 40s, when our careers have really started to take off—and we and the kids want more space from each other!

Vacation homes (Figure 2.3) are an interesting study. When we reach our peak spending years in our late 40s and early 50s, some of us buy that vacation house at the lake or the timeshare in Mexico we always wanted, and there is a clear peak in vacation home purchases around the age of 49. But for others, the vacation home comes later, at or near retirement. There is a secondary peak around the age of 67.

These are really two separate markets. The first is a vacation "getaway" house to be used on long weekends; the sort of place your teenagers might enjoy jet skiing at the lake. The second is more of a permanent home in which to live in retirement. Sometimes, these two markets overlap; there are plenty of resort communities that appeal to both weekend vacationers and to retirees looking to make a permanent move. And at the same time, there are plenty of communities that appeal to only one group or the other. If you plan to make an investment in this area, make sure you understand the demographics of the community because it could make the difference between scoring a home-run investment and losing a lot of money unnecessarily. Not everyone follows this real estate life cycle script exactly. Some of us get married earlier or later… or choose to remain single. Many Americans either can't afford to own a home or they live in a city where homeownership tends to be impractical or unaffordable to all but the wealthy, such as in New York City. And some of us choose to buy a single house and live in it our entire adult lives. But Figure 2.2 gives an accurate timeline of the average upper-middle-class American consumer and I consider it an accurate roadmap for the years ahead.

Let's dig deeper into the Consumer Expenditure Survey data to see what insights we can glean.

The total dollars spent on rent (Figure 2.4) peak at age 26 and then go into a steep decline that lasts pretty well for the rest of our lives. Tenant insurance (Figure 2.5) peaks at 29–30, though the drop-off is less pronounced and levels off by age 40. This makes intuitive sense. Those Americans who choose to rent in their 40s are more likely to have property worth insuring than a 20-something renter fresh out of school with furniture from Wal-Mart or Ikea. Renting and services relating to renting is still something that is oriented towards the young, however.

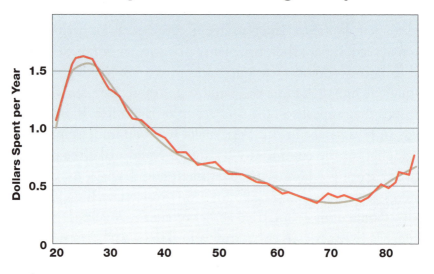

Figure 2.4

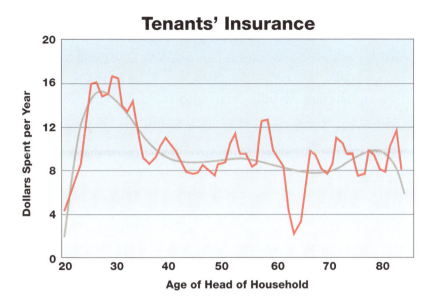

Figure 2.5

Right now, the rental market is hot, even in a down economy and should continue to be until at least 2017. The financial media credit this to a lousy housing market with tight credit. In other words, millions of Americans are renting because they cannot qualify for a mortgage, they cannot afford a house, or they are simply afraid of the housing market and prefer the flexibility of renting.

All of this is true, of course. The wave of foreclosures turned millions of homeowners into renters with bad credit. But this completely ignores the elephant in the room: the massive generation we call the Echo Boomers.

Look back at the Immigration-Adjusted Birth Index. There was a massive wave of births that crested in 1990, and those babies are today's 23-year-olds. So, even if we had never had a housing bust, we would have still had a massive boom in rental demand. The demographic trends were baked in more than two decades ago.

As an investor, are there still opportunities in rental apartments? Yes, there are, but the easy money has already been made. And over the next seven years, the waves of new renters coming down the pipeline will get progressively smaller. The only caveat here would be a pronounced new trend of young families renting longer and avoiding home ownership in a bad economy, which could last into the early 2020s.

Remember, after 1990, births went into a sharp decline that lasted until 1997. Those babies born in 1997 are today's high school kids… the college kids of 2016… and the new apartment renters from 2024 forward. Are you learning how to follow the moving parts yet? Don't worry, you will.

It is not that rental apartment demand will shrink, per se, but rather that its rate of growth will slow, at least at the national level. The cities experiencing the most growth and attracting the greatest number of new graduates may continue to enjoy a healthy rental market for years to come.

So, if you are an investor looking to allocate capital to the rental apartment market, you have to ask yourself a few questions and you need to have credible answers.

1. Is the city I am considering for rental investment attracting young people from other parts of the country?
2. Have developers already anticipated this and created an oversupply of new apartment properties?

Before you invest a single dime in apartments, have credible answers to these questions.

Moving on, let's take a look at what the Consumer Expenditure Survey can tell us about owned homes starting with interest paid.

In figures 2.6 and 2.7 we see very different age profiles for regular mortgage interest and interest on home equity loans. Spending on regular home mortgage interest peaks around age 41–42, in line with the peak for trade-up home purchases. This is precisely what we would expect.

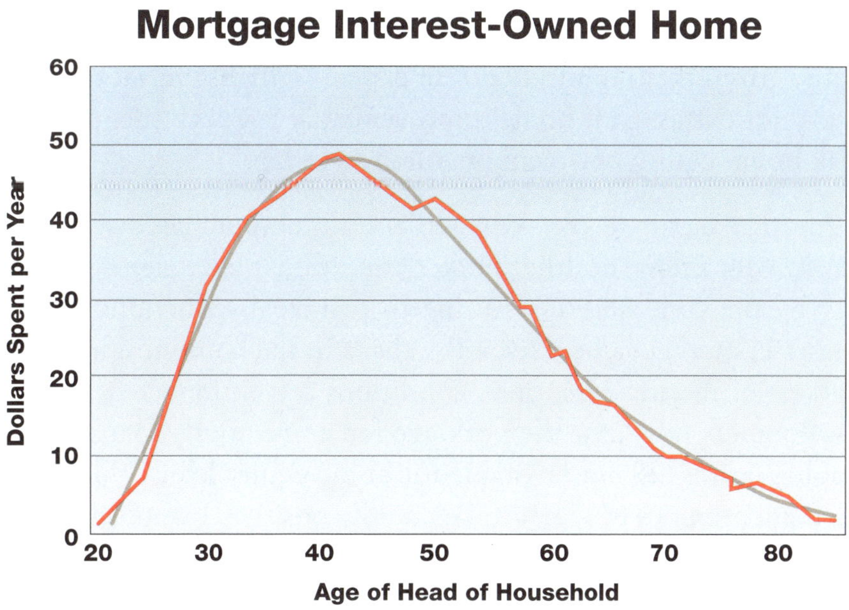

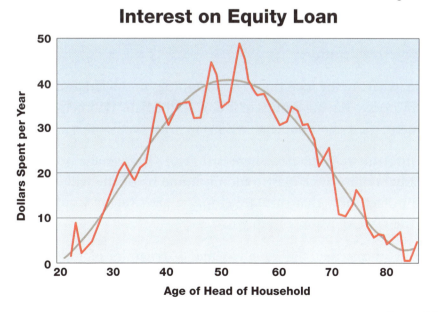

Figure 2.6

Figure 2.7

Interest on home equity loans peaks significantly later, at age 53, more in line with overall peak spending in the early 50s and college costs. Again, this makes sense. Particularly during the last boom, Americans took to using their homes as ATM machines, "extracting equity" from them to meet current expenses, high-end vacations, or to pay for extravagant home improvements. So, peak spending and peak home-equity borrowing naturally overlap.

Another factor to consider is that a home purchased when you are 40 will, under healthy market conditions, have significant equity by the time you are 50 due to principal reductions and increases in market value. Given the chaos in the home and mortgage markets of recent years, these conditions are no longer true. With the Boomers now past the peak age for home equity loans, demographic trends are not favorable for home equity loans. But even if the demographics were neutral or mildly positive, I wouldn't expect home equity lending to be a great business going forward. Nationwide, Americans lack the equity to make it work, and those that do have a lot of equity in their homes are too rattled and risk averse to borrow. Bottom line, I wouldn't be considering a career in home equity loan brokering. I expect this to be a business in decline for the foreseeable future.

So, what are the investment opportunities in single-family homes? There are two buying groups to follow — the Baby Boomers and their children, the Echo Boomers. We'll start with the Boomers.

Unfortunately, the news here isn't great. The average Boomer has already bought the largest trade-up home he or she will ever own. And in fact, now that they are empty nesters, many would love to sell their McMansion and downsize.

This means that the supply/demand dynamics of the high-end suburban home market are severely out of whack. The largest and richest generation in history is a net seller, while Generation X is too small to pick up the slack and Generation Y is too young and lacks the income to buy a high-end home. So, do not consider buying a McMansion for investment purposes. Don't do it. You will regret it. You may get what you think is a good price today from a motivated seller. But what makes you think that you're be able to sell it for a better price? Also, McMansions are risky as a "flip," and they are generally a bad choice as a rental as well. People who rent homes usually do so because they cannot afford to buy or because they are young and tend to move from job to job. Renters generally go for starter homes, not McMansions. Bottom line: Stay away from the McMansion market. And if you are thinking of downsizing to a smaller home, do it now rather than later as the larger home is likely to depreciate more than the smaller home in the years and decade ahead.

I would say that it is a little late in the game to be investing in vacation and resort homes as well, or at least those that do not cater to a retired crowd. As I discussed earlier in the commentary on Figure 2.3, vacation home spending has an initial peak at age 49, which the Baby Boomers have now passed. But the one area that could still benefit from Boomer spending is the retirement home market, which peaks at 67, and, to some extent, townhomes that are located closer to downtown areas. Many Boomers will continue to live in their current suburban home because they like the neighborhood and they have roots in the area. But for other Boomers, becoming an empty nester is an opportunity to escape the sterility and isolation of the suburbs, not to mention a chance to lower their property taxes and utility bills. Suburban subdivisions, while kid friendly, offer little in the way of amenities for active adults in their 50s and 60s. Many Boomers will find an urban townhouse within walking distance to shops and restaurants or resort and exurban communities with community centers designed for mingling with neighbors to be preferable.

We have two seemingly contradictory trends happening at the same time. After decades of urban decay, many American cities are "reurbanizing" with new residential and retail development tailored to a mostly high-income crowd of singles, marrieds without children, marrieds who can afford private school, and empty nesters. But at the same time, there is demand at the fringes of the city for both young families and active empty nesters who want a property that comes with a recreational lifestyle.

The areas now stuck in a demographic no-man's land of sorts are the suburbs built from the 1970s to the early 2000s. The decay we saw in America's urban inner cities after the 1960s was due to a lack of investment and high-income flight to these suburban areas. But as demographics and buying patterns shift, it is these suburbs that will suffer from lack of investment and high-income flight. Rather than having metro areas with a thriving periphery and a stagnating core, we have something that looks like a bullseye. A vibrant core and a vibrant fringe ring with decay in a large middle ring.

All cities have their unique characteristics, and there will be neighborhoods that buck these trends. But as a general rule, as an investor you will want to stay away from these areas and focus instead on the areas that offer better growth prospects.

Before we move on to the Echo Boomers, I want to say one last thing about the Boomers. While their demand for housing and most housing-related items is in decline, there are certain complementary businesses for which Boomer demand remains strong. Take a look at Figure 2.8. Demand for homeowners insurance remains constant well into our 70s. Whether we own our house outright or we are still paying down the mortgage, we still need to insure our homes from disasters. So, if you are an insurance agent or financial advisor, keep this in mind as you plan your practice for the years ahead.

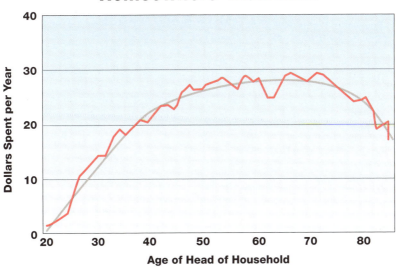

Figure 2.8

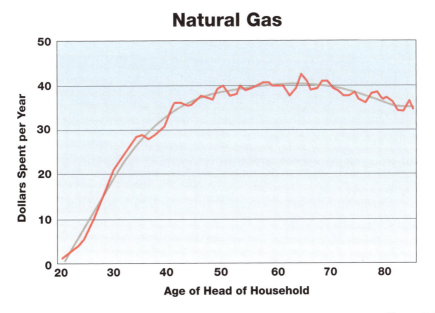

Figure 2.9

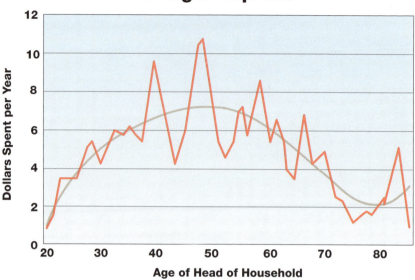

Figure 2.10

Likewise, basic utilities, such as natural gas, maintain a relatively constant demand (Figure 2.9). You still have to heat your home no matter how old you are and no matter how many kids live in the house. This is not really an investable area for most people, however, as utilities are provided by the city or by large corporations. There is not a lot of room for a would-be entrepreneur, unless you have a product or service that promises to save homeowners money on their heating and air conditioning bills, such as insulation or energy-efficient windows.

And finally, we come to moving expenses (Figure 2.10). This is a chart where using the smoothed trend line might be more instructive than using the raw data, as there are wild variations in the raw data from age 40 to age 60. In any event, the key point to take away is that spending peaks in the late 40s, or around 48.

I was initially surprised to see that expenses for moving, storage and freight peak in the late 40s, not too far before the overall peak in spending. I had assumed that the peak would come much sooner, as younger people tend to be more mobile and thus have higher and more frequent moving expenses.

The problem was that I didn't take that thought all the way to completion. Yes, younger people are more mobile. But they also have less "stuff." And what they do have, they are able to move themselves using a U-Haul trailer and their friends' arms and backs.

By the time people reach early middle age, they own more furniture and property and what they own is more valuable. Their time is also more valuable and their arms and backs more fragile. Few 45–50-year olds are willing to rent a U-Haul and move themselves unless they can use their children as slave labor!

Moving is a fairly easy business to start. All you need is a small fleet of leased trucks and a cheap workforce of young men willing to work part time. Unfortunately, the best time to start a moving business has already passed, and the demographic trends here are not favorable.

Now, on to the Echo Boomers. I've already touched on them several times in this chapter, but now it's time to get into the specifics. We know that the Echo Boomers are the next great generation. The question is: How do we profit from them?

As I mentioned earlier, it's too late to be making major investments in the apartment market. The largest cohort of the Echo Boomers is 23 years old and likely already rents an apartment. They may upgrade to nicer apartments and may ditch roommates as their incomes rise. But the simple fact is that they have already made the biggest impact they are going make on the apartment market.

The next major threshold for the Echo Boomers is the purchase of a starter home, which happens around the ages of 29–33, or as soon as you can afford it after having kids. The first wave of Echo Boomers is already in the early stages of a starter home boom that will extend into 2021–2022, but the difficult economy brings headwinds. The second wave will see its starter home boom in a better economy from around 2029 into 2038–2039.

This is a trend that we can get in front of by buying starter homes and renting them out with a goal of eventually selling out to an Echo Boomer family when the economy improves and they feel better about buying again. It's important to be very selective about properties you consider for purchase, however.

Right now, home prices have been stabilized by aggressive monetary stimulus by the Federal Reserve, by various distressed borrower programs sponsored by the federal government and by the government-sponsored enterprises such as Fannie Mae and Freddie Mac. Further, banks are strategically keeping foreclosed homes off the market to prevent a flood of supply from pushing prices lower. But none of these can be viewed as "sure things," and a change in any of the three could be disastrous for home prices.

Prices nationwide can still go much lower from current values, and in the areas where there is still high foreclosure inventory overhang an outright collapse in prices is not out of the question. And if the mortgage market seizes up again for any reason, then there is no telling where the bottom in prices might be.

There is still a lot of risk in this market, so it's important to get a good price. As with any investment, your returns ultimately depend on the price you pay, and it is important to have a margin of safety.

So, if you are considering building a portfolio of starter homes, keep these rules of thumb in mind. The investment absolutely must generate positive cash flow from the beginning. Determine what a realistic rental price would be based on other rental properties in the area. But to give yourself a decent margin of safety, assume that you might have to cut the rent by 20% or more if the economy takes another downturn or if the rental market in that neighborhood becomes oversupplied. If the expected rent is still enough to cover the mortgage, basic maintenance, and any other expenses, then the property is worth considering. If not, don't push it. Walk away and look for better investment opportunities elsewhere.

Secondly, find a motivated seller. It's still a buyer's market in most cities, and it makes no sense to waste time and resources haggling with a seller who has an unrealistic view of his home's worth. And along those lines, don't be afraid to make a low-ball offer. You lose nothing for trying, and if you offend the seller you can simply move on to the next house.

And finally, try to think as young parents would think. Does the neighborhood feed into a good school? Is it safe for children to play there? Remember, your ultimate goal is to sell the property to an Echo Boomer family down the road when the market improves again. They are your target market, so buy now what you expect they will be buying later. The next McMansion boom doesn't kick in until the first wave of Echo Boomers hits and the economy is expanding again around 2023 and such demand should stay strong until around 2032. That's well down the road and it's better to see how much excess inventory of suburban McMansions builds up in the decade ahead when younger couples are buying starter homes and older couples are trading down to urban townhomes.

With any investment or business venture, you have to keep the macro picture in mind because a sickly economy can disrupt even the most solid businesses. But this is even truer of real estate due to the leverage involved and the dependence on the credit markets. When banks aren't lending freely for mortgages, the demand for all housing sectors dries up in a hurry. So, while the demographic trends are very clear as to which sectors should do well and which sectors should do poorly, take the macro risk you face under consideration and give yourself an extra margin of safety. Unless a deal looks like a homerun, it's not a bad idea to sit it out. Other opportunities will present themselves.

Sports and Recreation

Sports and Recreation

Sports and recreation is a fairly broad category that covers a wide range of businesses and investment opportunities. In general, spending on sports and recreation tends to peak far earlier than overall peak spending, which is not a bad thing. It means that the Baby Boomers already peaked in their spending in these items years ago, so there is not a large crash to expect. There is, however, a new boom led by the Echo Boomers to look forward to.

By and large, an investment in a sports and recreation business opportunity will be a play on the tail end of Generation X and on the Echo Boomers and distinctly not on the Baby Boomers.

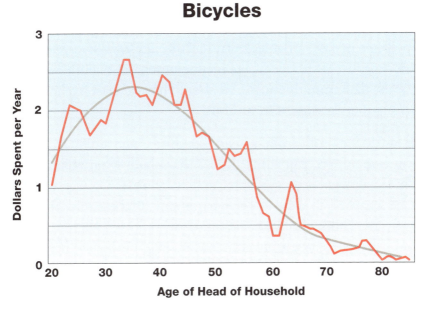

Figure 3.1

Let's start with a product that is part of every American's childhood, the bicycle (Figure 3.1). Spending on bicycles peaks at the ages of 33–34, and no, it is not because there are a lot of Lance Armstrong wannabes out there training for the Tour de France, nor is it due to 33-year olds becoming green activists who ditch their cars and pedal their way to work. Few 30-somethings are buying a bike for themselves. It's for their young children.

Let's do the math. If you have a child in your mid-to-late 20s, that child is going to be 5–10 years old by the time you hit your mid-30s. That's plenty old to be getting a nice bicycle for Christmas.

Demographic trends suggest that demand for bicycles should be strong for the next several years. Think back to the Immigration-Adjusted Birth Index. Subtracting 34 years from 2013 would put us in 1979, at the very tail end of Generation X and just before the birth explosion of the Echo Boomers. The number of Americans in their 30s will be rising for a long time to come.

Looking at the data another way, there was a surge in births that topped out in 2007. Babies born in 2007 are now five years old in 2013… or just at the age where bicycle purchases make sense. Looking at the data from this angle, we should have at least five more years of strong bicycle sales in front of us.

How do we profit from a trend like this? Open a bike store? Well, that is one option. But think deeper than that. What about starting an Internet business that sells stylish bike helmets? Or accessories that can be attached to a bike? Or what about offering bike riding lessons for the children of busy executives who don't have time to teach them? There are endless possibilities for small businesses here.

Moving on, Figure 3.2 shows demand for camping equipment. The story here is much the same. Demand has an initial peak at 41 and a secondary peak at 46, and it is not because urban city slickers have started to crave the great outdoors at that age. Again, it is due to children. When your son or daughter is 10–15 years old, it is the perfect time to take them camping. Or they may go without you with an organization such as the Boy Scouts or their local church youth group.

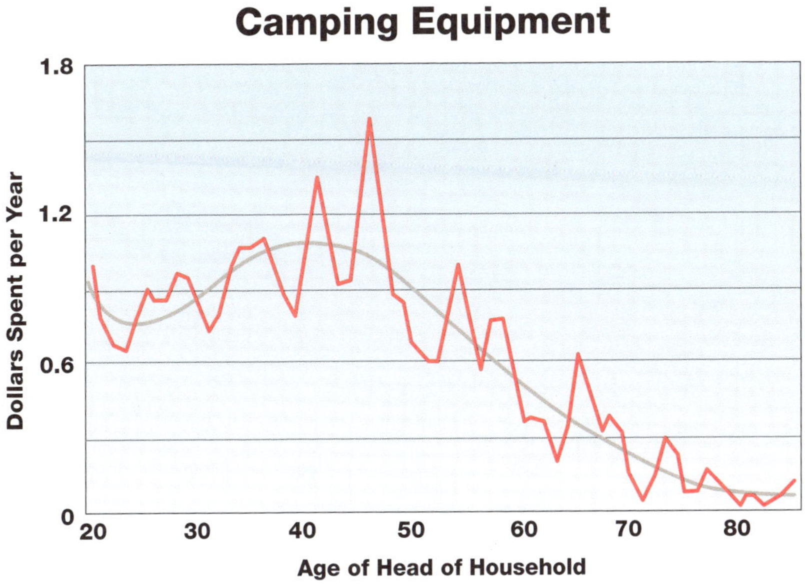
Camping Equipment
1.8
1.2
0.6
0
Dollars Spent per Year
20
30
40
50
60
70
80
Age of Head of Household

Figure 3.2

Focusing on the initial peak at 41, demographics are not unfavorable, though your strongest demand is still several years away, in the late 2020s. But if a camping-related business interests you, this is a good time to be laying the foundations and establishing your presence.

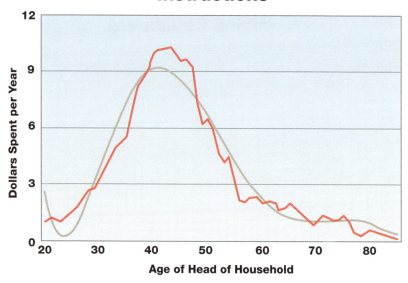

Figure 3.3

For a very pronounced demographic curve, look at Figure 3.3, which tracks fees for recreational lessons. There is a huge bulge in the early 40s that peaks in a rounded top between the ages of 40 and 44 and, again, it's not that 40-something Americans suddenly yearn to learn a new sport. Aside from perhaps golf or skiing lessons, we're done paying for sports lessons long before we reach adulthood. Rather, these lessons are for our kids.

In the immediate future, the best opportunities here are in serving the large cohort of children that peaked in 2007. The opportunities here are endless. Parents, and particularly higher-income parents, are competitive and are willing to pay for lessons for everything. Ballet, basketball, guitar, ice skating… you name it, and chances are good that there is a parent willing to pay for it.

The window here is fairly tight. By the time kids reach their teenage years, they've found a niche, be it the clarinet or competitive chess, and their interests get narrower. But again, we have many years in front of us before that becomes a problem.

Demand for water-sports equipment (Figure 3.4) takes an interesting shape. Demand rises to an initial peak at 39, fluctuates, and then has a sharp peak at 53. In a case like this, where the data is choppy, the trend line is going to be your best estimate.

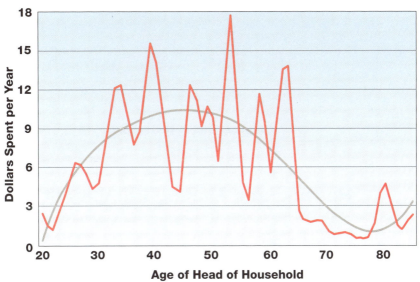

Figure 3.4

The key here is that demand rises sharply throughout the 20s and 30s, making this an ideal area to target the growing incomes of the Echo Boomers. If you live near a popular lake or beach, this is an area of opportunity.

Winter-sports equipment (Figure 3.5) is another area with promise. Demand turns up in the mid-20s and stays strong through the early 40s, where it has a sharp peak at age 41. If the Echo Boomers embrace skiing and snowboarding like previous generations, then demand for winter sports equipment should be very strong over the next 15 years or more.

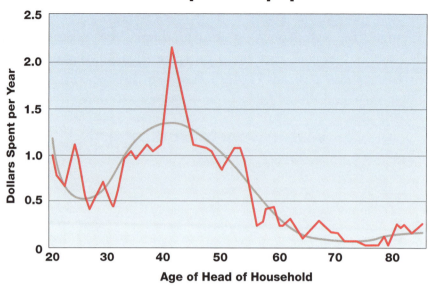

Figure 3.5

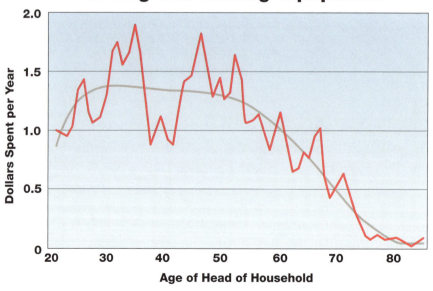

Figure 3.6

Hunting and fishing (Figure 3.6) are sports that exhibit less extreme characteristics. Demand has a peak around age 34, and a secondary peak around age 46. Looking at the smoothed trend line, the takeaway is that the real drop-off in demand happens after the early 50s.

The good news for businesses in this segment is that aging Boomers should be more or less replaced by up-and-coming Echo Boomers. This is not a major area for growth, but if your business concerns hunting and fishing, I can at least say that it should be fairly stable in the years ahead.

One caveat here is the regulatory environment. Fear that new gun control regulations are coming has led to an explosion of gun sales in 2012 and 2013. So, some of the sales happening today might reduce demand for guns in future years, as that demand is being pulled forward.

It may seem somewhat backward, but laws put in place to restrict firearms purchases often have the exact opposite results in the short term, as would-be buyers rush to make purchases today that they fear will be impossible or difficult tomorrow.

But this short-term distortion aside, we do not see increased gun control having a major impact on gun sales for hunting or sporting purposes. The impact, to the extent that there is an impact at all, will likely affect guns sold for self-defense or assault rifles; however, these can generally be modified into legally compliant guns with only minor modifications.

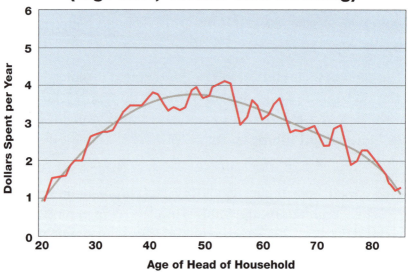

Figure 3.7

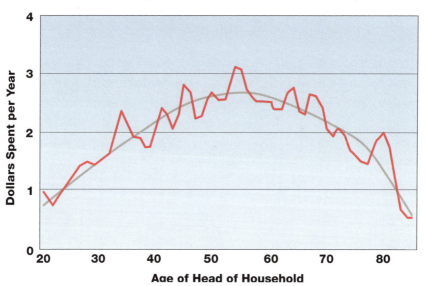

Figure 3.8

Fees for sports such as golf, tennis and bowling (Figure 3.7) peak in our early 50s, around 53, and membership fees for country clubs and other private-member clubs (Figure 3.8) peak around the same time, at age 54.

This does not bode well for these industries. The Baby Boomers are just peaking in their spending in these categories, and there is nowhere to go but down. The Echo Boomers will not be replacing their spending anytime soon. Bad demographics and a weak economy should mean lean times for these businesses for the next decade.

If you operate in a sports and recreation business or you are considering starting a business in this area, the key takeaway here is that your core customer is not a Baby Boomer. You are looking at cutting your teeth in selling to Generation X with a goal of expanding your sales to the up-and-coming Echo Boomers.

This page intentionally left blank.

Media

MEDIA

Media is a business area that is in a state of flux at the moment as the Internet and communications revolution has turned all media-related industries upside down. Until 12 years ago, there was no such thing as an iPod, and until 2007 there was no such thing as an Amazon Kindle. Up until very recently, the idea of watching TV shows on your computer would have been laughable to anyone other than a starving college student.

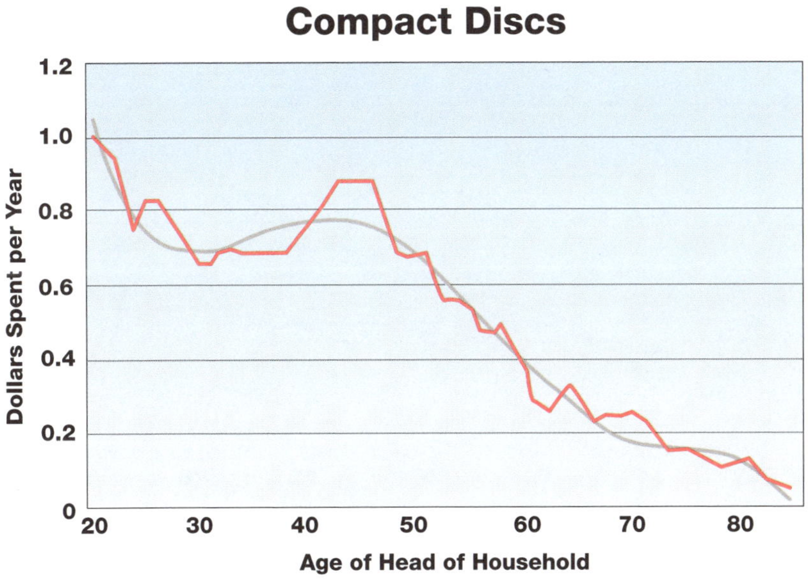
Compact Discs
Dollars Spent per Year
1.2
1.0
0.8
0.6
0.4
0.2
0
20
30
40
50
60
70
80
Age of Head of Household

Figure 4.1

So, media consumption is an area where technology changes will trump demographic trends and in which things are changing so fast that historical demographic analysis is dated by the time it is produced. It really doesn't matter when the peak spending age for compact discs is (Figure 4.1) because the compact disc as a media format is quickly becoming obsolete.

In fact, looking at Figure 4.1 will cause you to draw the wrong conclusion. While historically young people have been the largest consumers of music, today most of what they listen to is pirated online. The more honest 20- and 30-somethings buy their music online via iTunes, Amazon.com or some competing service. But the profit model itself is shot. If you want to sell compact discs, your best option is an older crowd who is less comfortable with technology even though historically this is a weaker demographic for music sales.

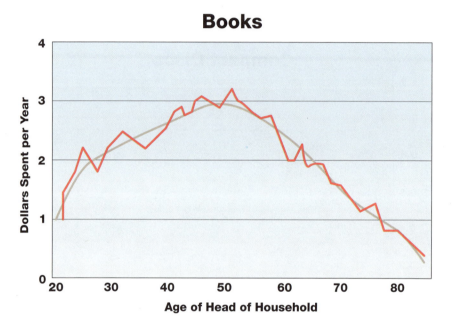

Figure 4.2

Books are another area undergoing a major upheaval. It is bad enough for the industry that peak spending on books is around age 51, which means that the Boomers are no longer a source of growth. But the much bigger issue is the rise of Internet sellers like Amazon.com, which more or less singlehandedly put Borders Books out of business and has Barnes & Noble on the ropes. And even bigger than this trend is the move away from paper books into electronic books.

Unless you own a specialty bookstore or web site that trades in antiques or some area of the book market that the big retailers are not serving, do not even consider books as a business. You would be putting yourself in direct competition with Amazon and Apple, and that is not a battle you are likely to win.

But there are other factors as well. The Internet has reduced the need for the traditional publishing apparatus altogether. Using print-on-demand publishing, which reduces the need for a large print inventory, or publishing as an e-book allows up-and-coming authors to skip the middleman and sell directly to their readers.

The process has empowered authors and turned them into entrepreneurs, which is a good thing. But it's leaving a burnt-out shell where the traditional publishing industry used to be.

If you work in the traditional publishing business, it may be time to pursue other options. A good editor can work as a freelancer for newly independent authors, and there will continue to be demand for marketing consultants, agents, and other middlemen that can help authors reach their goals. But you will be fighting for those jobs with the legions of unemployed editors from the large publishing houses that will continue to downsize in the years ahead. Frankly, this is a terrible business to be in.

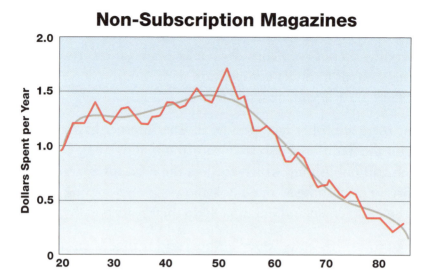

Figure 4.3

The same is true of magazines purchased off the rack (Figure 4.3). This is an expense that traditionally drops off after the age of 50. But widespread use of smartphones and tablet computers has absolutely gutted the business.

Think about it. Travelers would typically buy a magazine at the train station, airport, or perhaps at the supermarket as something to read to pass the time while waiting. Smartphones and tablets have absolutely killed these kinds of purchases.

Magazine subscriptions and newspaper subscriptions (Figures 4.4 and 4.5) are products that historically had peak demand far later in life than most. Magazine subscriptions peak and plateau from 63 to 67 and newspapers nearly 10 years later.

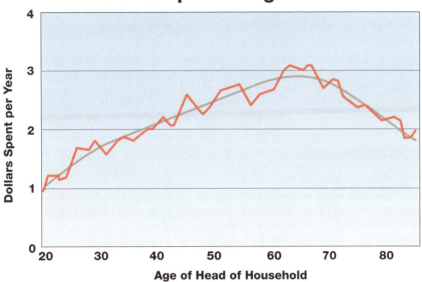

Figure 4.4

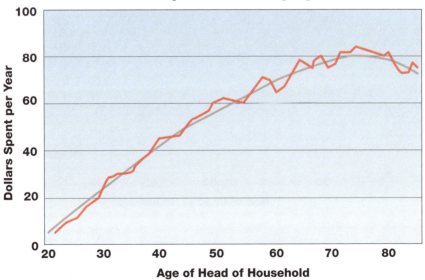

Figure 4.5

But does this mean that aging Baby Boomers will provide a reprieve to these ailing industries? Not likely. Boomers are getting more of their content online, and this will only continue to increase.

And what about media that tends to be consumed by younger consumers, such as movie rentals? (Figure 4.6) Demand here has traditionally been pretty stable from the mid-20s to the early 40s.

But this too is a difficult area for an aspiring entrepreneur. Your first problem is rampant piracy. But beyond this, the DVD format is in decline, and at this point the only viable models seems to be the Redbox kiosk and, to some extent, the Netflix DVD-by-mail model. Opening a rental store would be financial suicide; if Blockbuster can't make it work, chances are good that you won't be able to either.

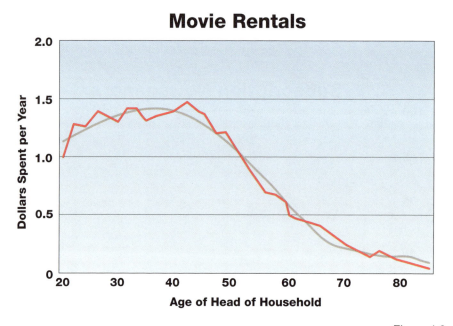

Figure 4.6

Otherwise, what are your options? Online streaming services are already offered by heavyweights like Apple, Netflix, Amazon and even Wal-Mart via its Vudu service. Unless you are a computer programmer with a radical new innovation, it is hard to see much potential for small business operators in this space.

I've painted a rather bleak picture of media industries, and I hope you take my warnings seriously. It is generally a mistake to stake your future on a highly competitive industry that also happens to be in a major state of flux. As a general rule, media businesses are best avoided.

This page intentionally left blank.

Furniture and Appliances

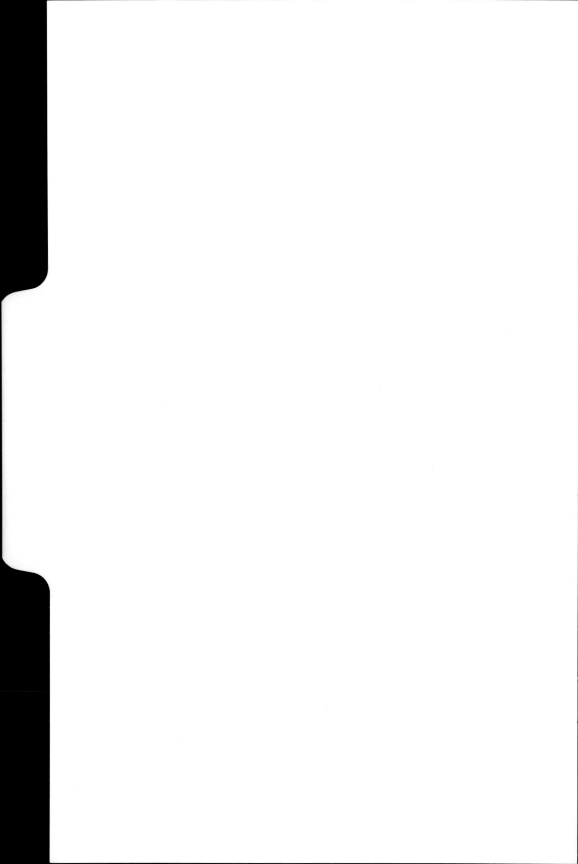

FURNITURE AND APPLIANCES

Furniture and appliances fall into a special category of expenses along with autos and real estate in that they are often financed. This means that macro forces, such as interest rates and ease of credit, have an effect on sales. Demand for furniture and appliances is also tied to real estate in that the purchase of a new house often spurs a spending spree on items to fill it up.

So, while furniture and appliances are directly affected by demographic forces, they are also indirectly affected by these knock-on effects.

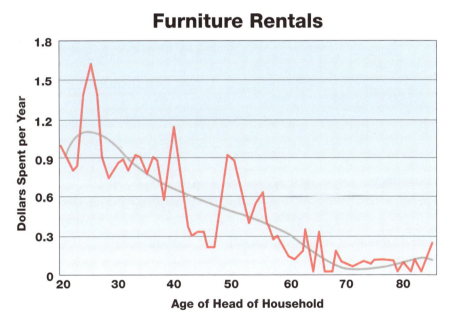

Figure 5.1

With that said, let's jump into it, starting with furniture rental (Figure 5.1). Perhaps not too surprisingly, furniture rental is generally for young people. The chart is choppy, but it tells a story that makes sense. Demand peaks around age 25 and continues in a downward slope until it bottoms out at close to zero. I do not expect furniture rental to be a growth business for the next several years. I would lump it in with other college-era expenditures (see Chapter 1).

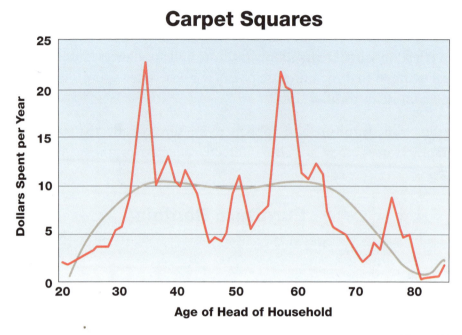

Figure 5.2

I'm always impressed with the level of detail in the Consumer Expenditure Survey. Yes, as you can see in Figure 5.2, the government even tracks the sales of carpet squares. I included this chart in the interest of being thorough, but I don't see much in the way of opportunity here. Though if you happen to own a store that sells throw rugs or carpets, you will be happy to know that demand for your products should be strong in the years ahead.

Moving on to more significant household items, let's take a look at sofas, living room chairs, and living room tables (Figures 5.3, 5.4 and 5.5).

You may naturally think that all three would have very similar demand characteristics and that they were purchased at the same time, but this is not the case at all. Sofa and table buying have an initial peak around 30 years old with later demand spikes in the mid-40s and again in the mid-50s. Demand really starts falling in the late 50s and early 60s.

Yet bucking this trend, living room chairs have a fairly steady rising demand until it spikes at age 57 and hangs on until a steady decline in the mid-60s.

Why the difference in buying patterns? I would surmise that as people age and spend more time in their homes, they want to be comfortable, and a La-Z-Boy recliner is more comfortable for quiet nights at home enjoying a movie than a sofa. They offer better back support, which is going to be attractive to a person in their 50s or 60s, especially relative to a person in their 20s or 30s.

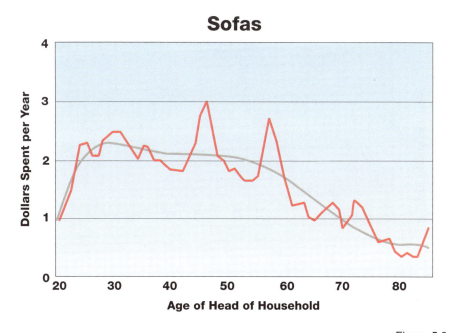

Figure 5.3

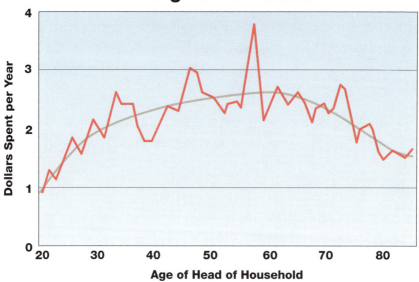

Figure 5.4

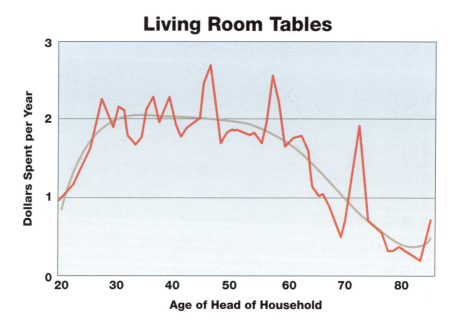

Figure 5.5

The demographic forecast for living room furniture is mixed. All else being equal, rising demand for sofas and coffee tables by the Echo Boomers should almost be high enough to compensate for falling demand from the Baby Boomers. But all else isn't equal and the housing market and economy remain depressed. Demand for living room chairs should be strong, but probably not strong enough to warrant starting a new business based on chairs.

Moving out of the living room, we see that demand for mattresses and springs (Figure 5.6) follows a similar pattern as sofas and coffee tables though with a slightly later drop-off in demand. There is a large surge leading into the age of first home purchase, around 31–32, after which demand levels off. Spending has a series of peaks at 25, 32, and 46 and starts to decline in a big way after a final peak in the early 60s.

At the risk of being crass, it is worth revisiting my comments from the introduction that economics is based on sex. The mattress market is not uniform. While overall spending is higher in the late 20s and early 30s as young couples furnish their new homes, when consumers in their 50s and 60s buy, they tend to spend more. They buy a different type of product, however.

Last year, *Barron's Magazine* ran a story titled "Sex or Sleep" in which they outline the economics of memory foam mattresses such as those made by Tempur-Pedic.[13] Memory foam mattresses tend to be unpopular with younger couples because they are seen as being an impediment to romantic life. But for the Baby Boomer buyers of Tempur-Pedic mattresses, this is apparently something they are willing to sacrifice for a good night's sleep.

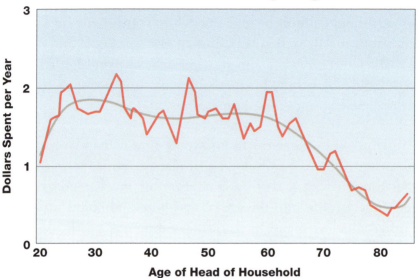

Figure 5.6

In any event, mattresses should be a fairly stable business in the years ahead. Family formation by the Echo Boomers should lead a broad-based rally, whereas trade-up buying by the Baby Boomers should continue for the remainder of this decade.

Again, any new shocks to the housing market or to the economy will hurt bed sales. When money is tight, buying a luxurious new bed is not a high priority. But as far as the furniture market goes, mattresses are not a bad product area for the years ahead.

I can't say the same for office furniture for home use (Figure 5.7), which has a jagged series of peaks starting from age 43 to 58. Overall, I am not particularly enthusiastic about the market for office furniture. The Echo Boomers are already well on their way to being incorporated into the workforce, meaning that companies have already had to build out more office space and buy the necessary furniture. Unemployment remains high, and any improvement in the economy that leads to new hiring might require new office furniture purchases.

But at the same time, the Baby Boomers have just now started what will be the largest retirement wave in history, one that won't peak until 2025 or later. Overall, the prognosis for office furniture retailers is not particularly good. Office furniture for home use has better demographic trends, as you can see in the graph. But given that this is only a subset of a larger market (and one that has very negative demographic trends) I would stay away from this business.

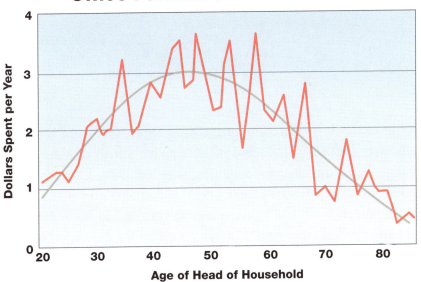

Figure 5.7

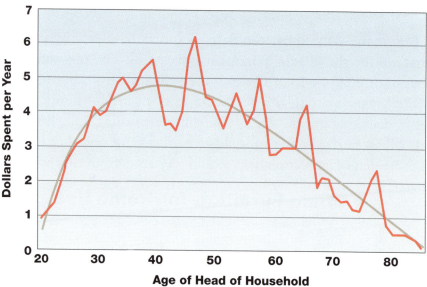

Figure 5.8

The outlook for kitchen and dining room furniture looks a little better (Figure 5.8). Demand rises sharply into the late 30s and has a peak around age 46, meaning that the Baby Boomers already peaked in their spending here and the damage from their aging is already done. And the upward slope from 20 to 40 is far steeper than the downward slope from 40 to older. So, if you own a furniture store or are considering making an investment in the industry, it makes sense to orient your inventory to the tastes and preferences of the Echo Boomers. For the next 15–20 years, they are going to be your primary clientele.

Moving now away from furniture and into appliances, we see buying patterns that are a little peculiar. Clothes dryers (Figure 5.9) have a demand curve that loosely resembles that of sofas, coffee tables and beds, though everything seems to be pushed back by about 10 years. Demand has an initial peak around 37, but there is a higher peak at 45–46 with trade-up home buying. After this point, the graph gets a little choppy, making the trend line a better gauge of demand.

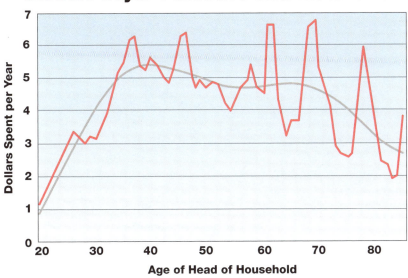

Figure 5.9

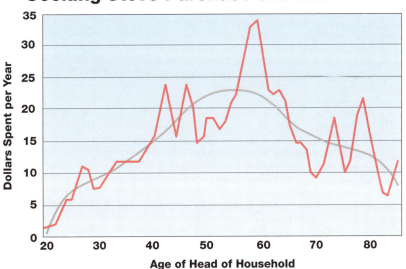

Figure 5.10

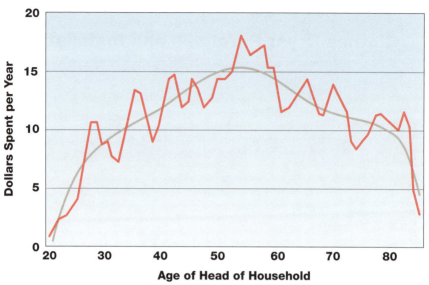

Figure 5.11

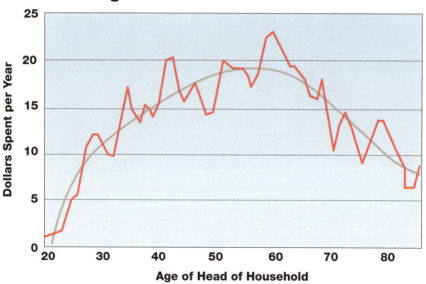

Figure 5.12

Cooking stoves, microwaves and refrigerators (Figures 5.10, 5.11 and 5.12) all have surprisingly late peak spending ages as well. Ovens peak around 58–59 and microwaves don't peak until around 54, when home improvements for kitchens and bathrooms are strong. Refrigerator spending doesn't peak until the ages of 58–60.

This implies that, all else being equal in the housing market, demand should remain relatively high for appliances for the next several years. The drop-off in demand from the Baby Boomers will not happen for another few years, while demand should rise from Echo Boomers who are starting their family lives. Moreover, there may also be pent-up demand from purchases that were postponed due to the bad economy of the past five years.

The advent of "smart appliances" that are connected to your home's Wi-Fi network also create interesting opportunities. Younger consumers are more comfortable with technology and with sharing personal information over the Internet, so Internet-enabled appliances should be an area of high growth in the years to come. Imagine being able to preheat your oven or to start a hot bath remotely from your smartphone using an iPhone or an Android app. The possibilities here are endless.

I have no specific recommendations as to which jobs or investment opportunities to pursue, but I would encourage you to brainstorm ways that you can profit from one of the major consumer trends of the coming decade: the networking of the American house and its appliances. If nothing else, network monitoring could be a profitable service business with regular, annuity-like income.

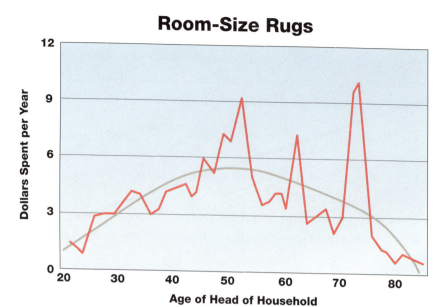

Figure 5.13

And we come to an end with large area rugs and other "non-permanent" floor coverings (Figure 5.13). Here, the outlook isn't good. The Baby Boomers just peaked in their spending on these items, and it will be a while before the Echo Boomers are able to pick up the slack. I would tend to ignore the large spike after the age of 70, as this would appear to be noise. Overall, this is an area I recommend avoiding.

For the aspiring entrepreneur, I see plenty of opportunities in the decade ahead in the furniture and appliances sphere. But the most promising development in my view is the smart, Internet enabled appliance and the possibilities for an automated house that this creates. Much like home security systems, networks need to be monitored. If you are technologically savvy, exploring business models based on this might have a lot of potential.

Home Goods

HOME GOODS

Let's take a look now at smaller household items. The products in this section are far less dependent on credit than furniture and appliances and tend to be relatively inexpensive. This makes them less susceptible to macro forces and to the broader state of the economy. New home sales (or a lack thereof) will have an effect on demand, but demographic trends will clearly dominate.

For many items in this category, the demographic picture is not good. Let's start with demand for bathroom and kitchen linens (Figures 6.1 and 6.2). Demand for bathroom linens has a rounded top from 46 to 57, while kitchen and dining linens has a sharper peak around 57, again a part of the home improvement trends after the kids leave the nest. Now it's your home.

The demand patterns here are interesting and not particularly intuitive. You might think that bathroom and kitchen linens would peak around the age of first marriage, in the late 20s, or at the age of first home purchase, but the data here is unambiguous. Spending on items such as towels and tablecloths rises well into the 50s.

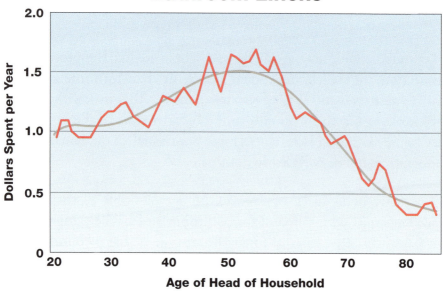

Figure 6.1

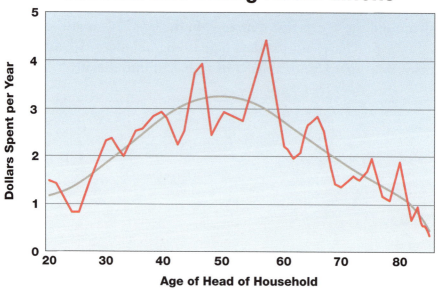

Figure 6.2

Bedroom Linens

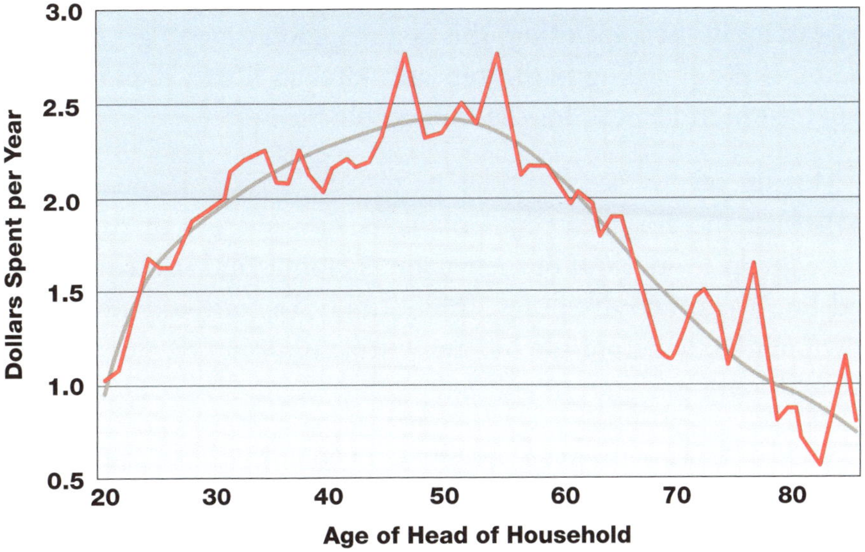

Figure 6.3

Slipcovers, Decorative Pillows and Cushions

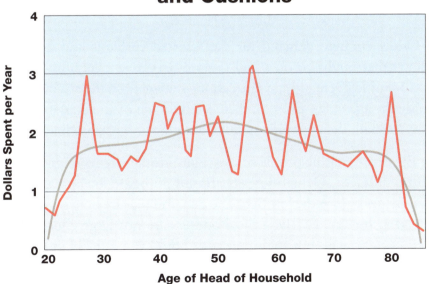

Figure 6.4

Call it the "Martha Stewart Living Wave," if you will, but the point here is obvious. With the Baby Boomers now already peaking or close to peaking in their spending, this is not a good time to get started in the business of selling bathroom and kitchen linens. Demand here may have seen its peak for the foreseeable future.

Moving on, we see a similar pattern in bedroom linens (Figure 6.3). Demand for sheets and blankets rises sharply in the 20s, as young people move out of their parents' homes and student housing and into their own dwellings. Interestingly, the rate of growth slows down markedly before age 30. Yet it still continues to grow past age 50, with twin peaks at 46 and 54.

Some of this is a matter of quality over quantity. A 50-year-old consumer will generally have a higher income than a 30-year-old consumer, all else being equal, and will be willing and able to spend more on a set of sheets. The older we get, the more we value a good night's sleep.

Still, the takeaway is the same. With the Boomers now in retreat, this is not a good time to be selling bed linens, or at least not high-end bed linens.

Oddly enough, demand for the assorted cushions and decorative pillows that might go on a bed (Figure 6.4) have a very different demand profile. Demand stays in a choppy range from the age of 25 until nearly the age of 80. Even so, there is not much of an investable theme here. Overall, demographic trends do not favor bedroom linens.

The demographic profile of closet and storage items (Figure 6.5) is a little different. Demand peaks around 35 before having a series of choppy peaks into the late 50s. The demand picture here is not nearly as bad as for linens. The Echo Boomers are not large consumers at their current ages, but their demand should rise quickly in the years ahead, as you can see from the steepness of the curve between the ages of 20 and 30. And any improvement in the housing market and the job market should allow for more mobile workers who relocate more often and have greater needs for items such as closet organizers. The key is looking for items that benefit from the family formation of the Echo Boomers.

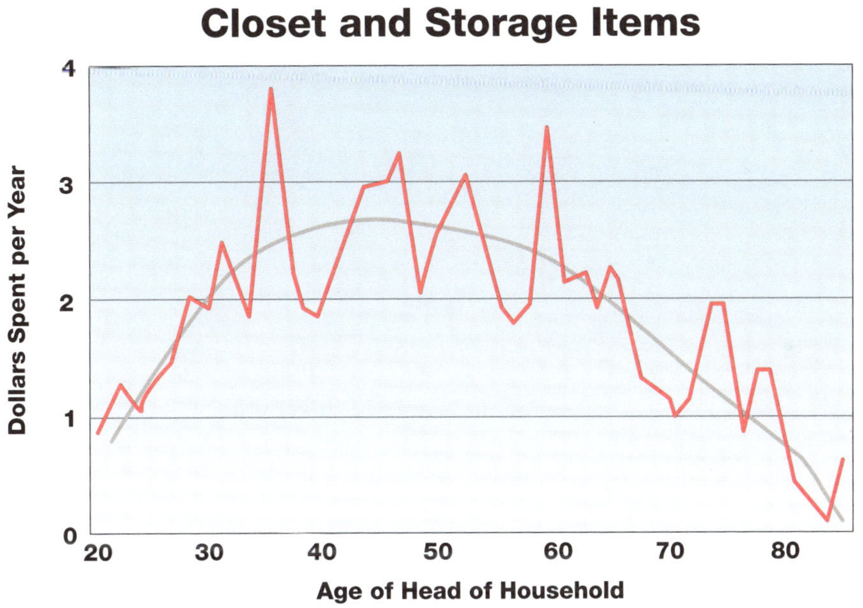

Closet and Storage Items

Figure 6.5

Perhaps a little strangely, curtains and drapes may be poised to do well (Figure 6.6). Demand initially peaks around the age of 40 but has a larger peak around 59. Based on these figures, these items are in a demographic sweet spot in that they won't be too terribly affected by a slowdown in Baby Boomer spending, yet they should also benefit from Echo Boomer spending.

The demand patterns for venetian blinds and window shades (Figure 6.7) suggest much of the same. Demand initially peaks a little earlier, around age 41, before a large spiked peak at 59. But the takeaway is the same. Home décor items that pertain to windows have a positive demographic outlook starting in a few years.

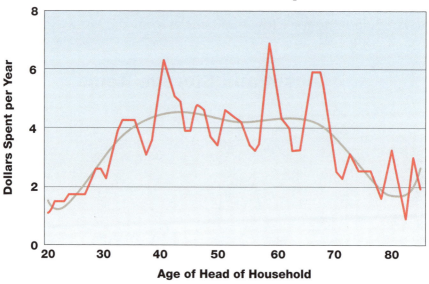

Figure 6.6

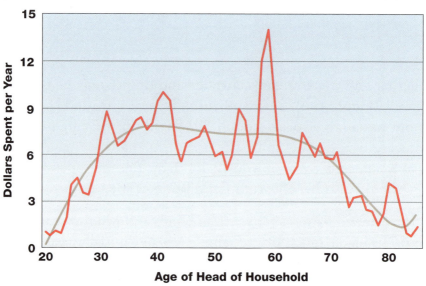

Figure 6.7

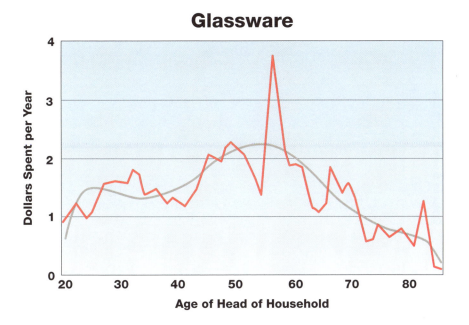

Figure 6.8

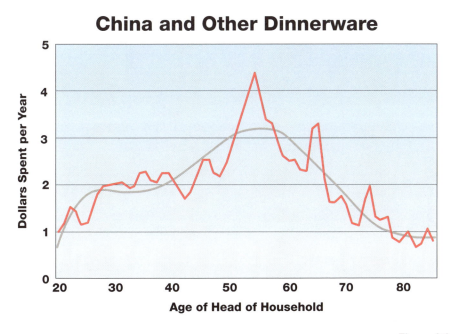

Figure 6.9

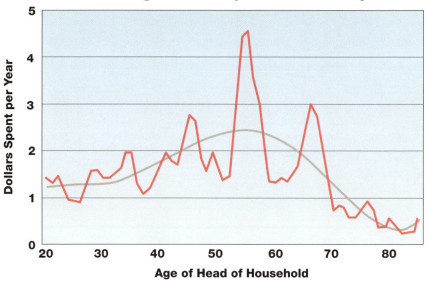

Figure 6.10

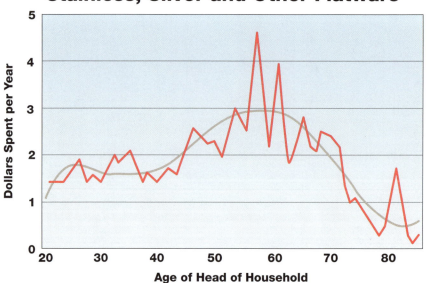

Figure 6.11

I have to admit I was a little surprised by the demand characteristics of glassware (Figure 6.8), china and other dinnerware (Figure 6.9), serving pieces other than silver (Figure 6.10) and flatware (Figure 6.11). I would have expected purchases of these items to correspond to marriage, yet demand for all do not peak until well into the 50s. Spending on glassware peaks around age 56, china at age 54, serving pieces at ages 54–55 and flatware at age 57.

While much of this is no doubt the result of empty nesters buying nice things for their homes once their children are no longer there to break them, it is possible that consumers over the age of 50 are buying some of these items as wedding presents for those same children. The Consumer Expenditure Survey does not give us any indication of who the intended recipient is, only the buyer.

What are we to glean from this? The Baby Boomers have a couple more years of strong spending left in them in these segments, but then their demand starts to fall off a cliff. That is not good news for stores that specialize in sales of these high-end home goods.

Overall, the trend here is not positive. To the extent that retailers have success here, it will be due to their ability to reach the Echo Boomers as they enter the marriage and family formation stage. Think of the next few years as being an investment in the future. The retailers that appeal to the up-and-coming Echo Boomers will benefit from years of rising growth. But those that depend on the tastes of aging Baby Boomers should see years of disappointing sales in front of them.

Anyone who picks up this book five to 10 years from now, might find it funny or even quaint that I included clocks (Figure 6.12). Apart from watches, which are more a fashion accessory than a functioning tool for telling the time, clocks are a product that is almost certainly in terminal decline. Younger consumers generally use the built-in alarm clock in their smartphone for their morning wake-up. And as market penetration and usage of smartphones increase, consumers further and further up the age scale will follow suit. Most consumers that use alarm clocks have had the same clock for years and use it more out of habit than anything else. Spending on clocks has an early peak around 40 and a much larger peak in the late 50s. But as smartphone usage increases, I expect the curve to shift further out to favor older ages. Still, given that this is a business in decline, I would not advise attempting to market clocks to aging Baby Boomers unless antiqued grandfather clocks become a trendy home décor item (stranger things have happened.)

Nor would I recommend a career as a florist. Demand for fresh flowers and potted plants peaks at age 55, and the largest numbers of Baby Boomers will pass this peak in just a couple years. Based on demographic factors alone, you would expect this business area to be in trouble. But making it worse for smaller businesses is the rise of online flower-buying options. Many of these sites act as "middlemen" between the consumer and the small neighborhood flower shop. But it still shows a lack of control on the part of the florists that make the business unappealing going forward.

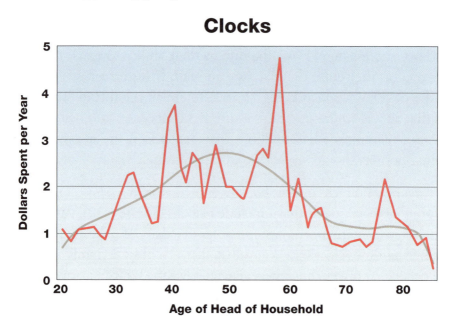

Figure 6.12

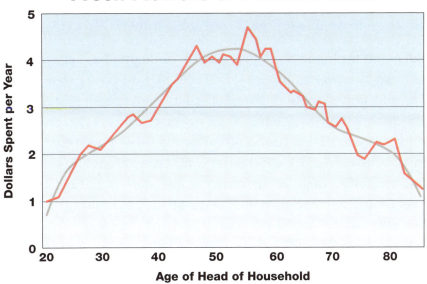

Figure 6.13

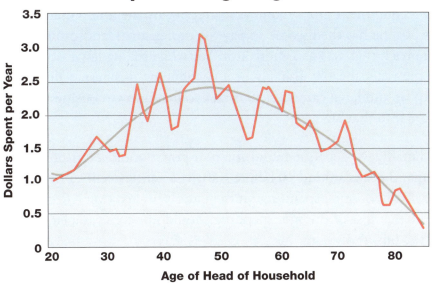

Figure 6.14

Demand for lamps and lighting fixtures (Figure 6.14) peaks around 47, not too long after the peak in trade-up home sales. Demand here looks to be in decline for the foreseeable future.

Demand for home products generally thought of as being "masculine" such as lawn equipment (Figure 6.15), non-power tools (Figure 6.16) and power tools (Figure 6.17) have interesting patterns. Demand for lawn mowing equipment peaks around 53–54, and power tools have twin peaks around 46–47 and 51. For power tools, this is fairly intuitive. Men have more time and more disposable income for home projects in their 50s than they would at an earlier age, and they also are more likely to own a large garage to put it all in. And given that power tools often have useful lives for decades, a man in his 70s who actively spends his free time on carpentry projects probably bought the tools decades before.

Lawn equipment is less intuitive. One would think that demand for lawn equipment would closely correlate with demand for starter homes. But one aspect is very intuitive, and that is that demand for lawn equipment drops like a rock after 50. By the time a man reaches his 50s, he has the income to pay for professional landscaping and a sore back that acts as a motivator. So, while selling lawn equipment in the years ahead will likely be a challenging business, selling landscaping and lawn care services is an excellent growth business. I'll get more into that later.

Finally, we get to demand for non-power tools. Non-power tool demand peaks around 30 before starting a gentle decline. This means that Baby Boomer spending on these tools peaked over a decade ago, so further loss of Boomer spending should not come as a large shock to the business.

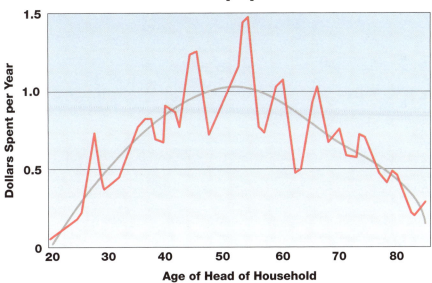

Figure 6.15

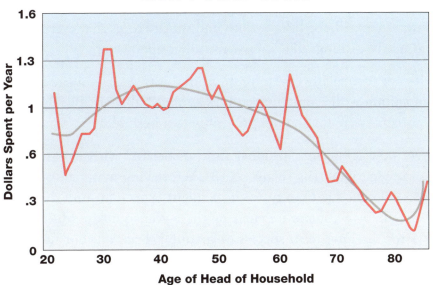

Figure 6.16

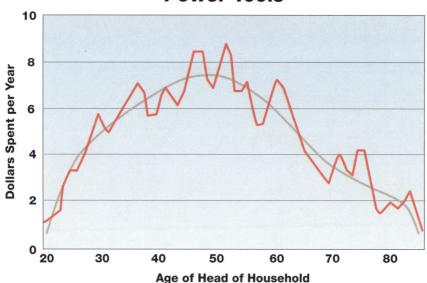

Figure 6.17

This is an area that should profit from the maturing and household formation of the Echo Boomers. As they get married and settle into homes, they will need the various and sundry tools that every household needs — things like screwdrivers, hammers, etc.

It's not particularly easy to profit from this trend, as you are in direct competition with Home Depot, Lowes, and Wal-Mart. But there may be potential here for an entrepreneur with a fresh idea.

We now come to a product most associated with elderly women — sewing materials (Figure 6.18). Yet, sewing materials peak at a much younger age than most of us might expect, around the age of 59. The Baby Boomers are entering these years quickly, which is bad news for the long-term success of Joanne Fabrics or your neighborhood sewing and fabric store.

Small electrical kitchen appliances (Figure 6.19) — things like blenders and coffee machines — peak a little earlier, around the age of 54. Again, this suggests that sales should be strong in the immediate future, but the forecast after that gets bleak.

Products that have done particularly well in this segment in recent years are those that appeal to higher-income consumers who live alone, such as a divorced Baby Boomer. A good example would be single-serving coffee and espresso machines, such as the Nestle Nespresso machine endorsed by the actor George Clooney. The demographic sweet spot for these kinds of appliances is the mid-to-late 50s—old enough to afford a lifestyle product like this, but young enough to try something new. Unfortunately, this window is quickly closing for the Baby Boomer generation. A would-be entrepreneur has only a few years left to take advantage of this trend.

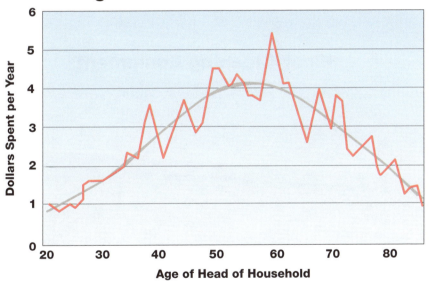

Figure 6.18

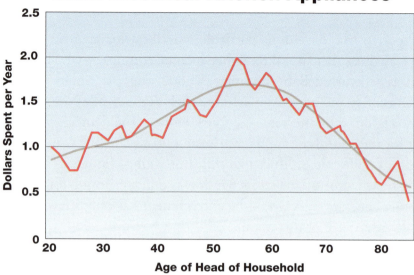

Figure 6.19

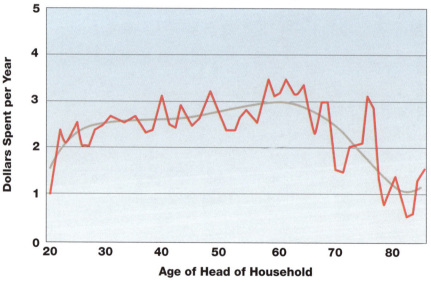

Figure 6.20

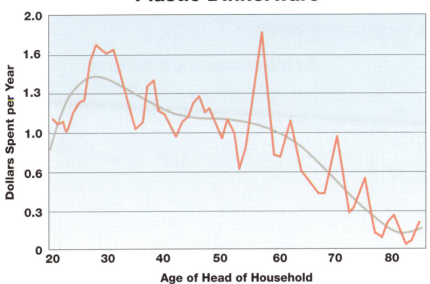

Figure 6.21

Moving into more obscure home products, demand for floor cleaning equipment (Figure 6.20) is remarkably stable from the mid-20s all the way into the 60s, with a peak around 61. This is a niche market and not one that most entrepreneurs would naturally gravitate towards. But, based on demographic trends, it is one that I would have to recommend for its stability. By the time the Baby Boomers age to the point of no longer needing these products, their children will be more than old enough to pick up the slack.

Plastic dinnerware (Figure 6.21) is a different story, however. Demand initially peaks at 28-31 and then plummets for the rest of our lives with the exception of one last spike in the late 50s.

This pattern surprised me when I first saw it. While few Americans outside of college students or young bachelors eat their meals with plastic forks and knives, I would expect demand to rise in the 30s and 40s for the lunchboxes of our school children. The data simply does not support this, however. The Echo Boomers will pass through the peak spending years for this product within the next few years, making this an area best avoided.

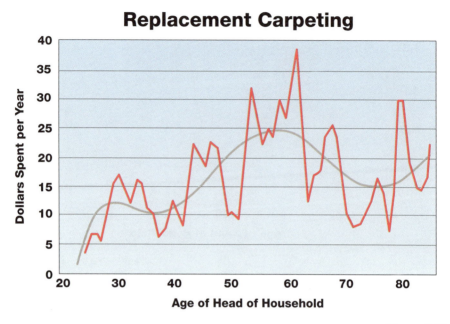

Figure 6.22

Replacement wall-to-wall carpeting (Figure 6.22) is an area that shows growth until nearly the age of 60. Based on demographics alone, the aging of the Baby Boomers should mean good things for the remainder of this decade.

This doesn't tell the full story, however. Remember, we are just coming out of the worst housing bust in modern American history, and millions of Americans are still underwater on their mortgages. Millions more are in some stage of foreclosure. As homes eventually get cycled back into the resale market, it should create a boom in demand for replacement carpet as the existing owners (or banks who own post-foreclosure) get the homes ready to sell. Carpet should be an even better business to be in than the demographics suggest, though demand may be weak for the next couple years.

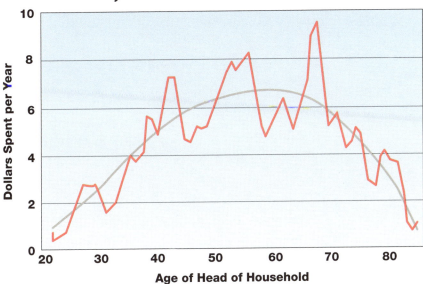

Figure 6.23

And finally, we come to wood, kerosene and other fuels (Figure 6.23). Demand for these fuels has a spike around the age of 67. I don't know how many proprietors of firewood happen to be reading this book, but for what it is worth, I would expect demand for your product to have stable demand for the next several years, weather and other factors being equal.

While there is variation among home products, the large majority have peak spending years that are very close to the peak for overall spending. This means that most of these products should follow the path of the Spending Wave, which means moribund demand for the next several years. To the best extent you can, it makes sense to reorient your business to prepare for the maturing of the Echo Boomers. You will have several lean years in front of you, but if you survive, you will be well placed for the boom to follow in the next decade.

This page intentionally left blank.

Home Services

Home Services

While the overall picture for home goods is not positive, the news for most home services is better. As Americans age, there are more tasks that they either cannot continue to do or that they prefer to pay someone else to do. With few exceptions, home services is an area I recommend to profit from the aging of the Baby Boomers, even in an environment of overall lower spending.

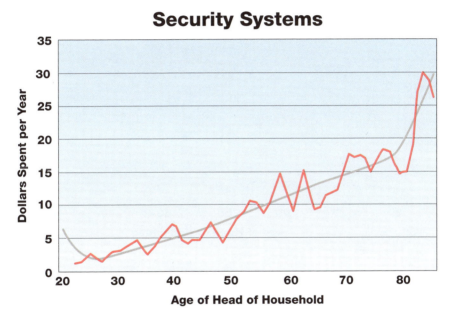

Figure 7.1

Let's start with home security systems and security guards (Figure 7.1). The older we get, the more vulnerable we feel and the more at risk we are to attack or robbery. Demand for home security increases every year from young adulthood to death.

This is an excellent area of opportunity. Starting a bodyguard or "rent a cop" service is unrealistic for the most part because the percentage of Americans that can afford private security is small. Home security system installation and monitoring is a very different story, however. Many of the large home security firms such as ADT use local resellers and technicians to install their systems. This could be an excellent business model for neighborhoods with large populations of Baby Boomers.

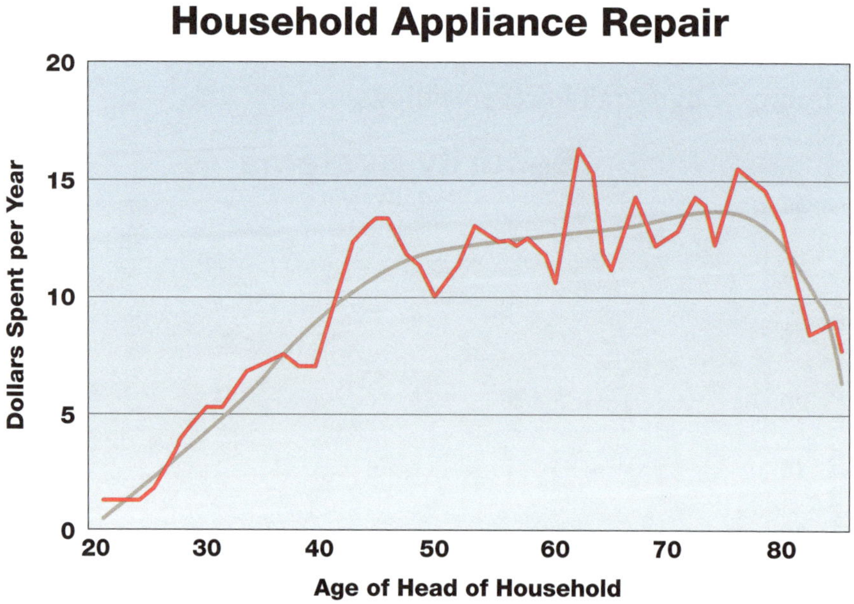

Household Appliance Repair

Figure 7.2

Remote monitoring of security cameras would also be a viable growth business, as would ongoing maintenance of existing security equipment.

Repair of household appliances (Figure 7.2) is also a booming business well into our 70s. After our peak spending years, we are far less likely to spend money on new white goods like washing machines and refrigerators. But we are definitely likely to repair what we already own after it breaks.

For Americans living on a fixed income, paying a nominal amount of money to repair a broken appliance is going to be far less of a financial burden than buying a new appliance altogether.

Demographic trends suggest that this will be a booming business opportunity for years, and that is just the start. The rise in popularity of new "smart" appliances means that appliance repair will be increasingly more sophisticated and specialized. This means that there will be boom in demand for highly skilled technicians with the knowhow to do the work.

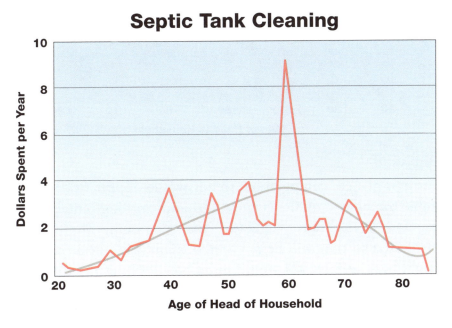

Figure 7.3

Demand for lower-tech home services — such as septic tank cleaning (Figure 7.3) — remains strong for longer than most products and services as well. Demand for septic tank cleaning has a massive peak around 60, after which it drops dramatically. It's important to understand the reasoning for this. It is not necessarily that those over the age of 60 use their plumbing less frequently but rather than they tend to own fewer properties that have a septic tank or they tend to visit those properties less frequently.

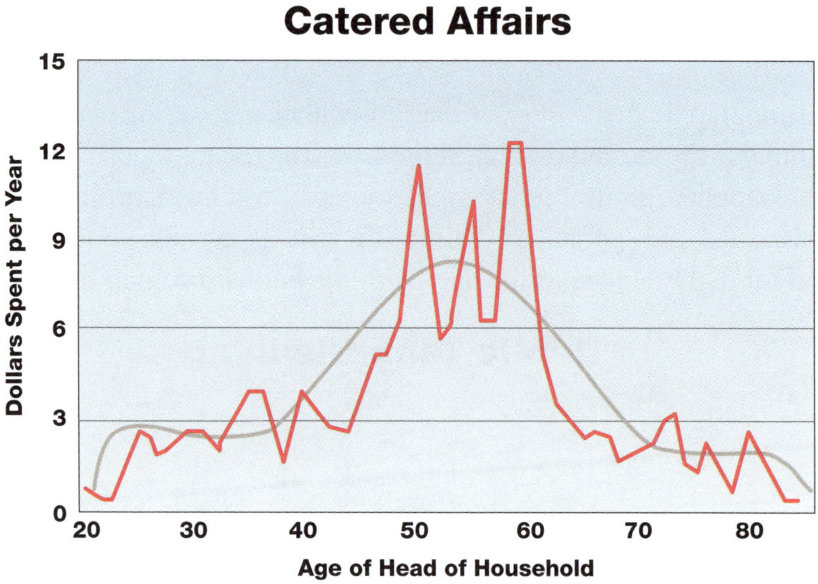

Catered Affairs

Figure 7.4

At first glance, demographic trends would appear to be less favorable for catered affairs (Figure 7.4) and clothing rental (Figure 7.5). Both have patterns suggesting that the Boomers have already contributed all they will here. Catered affairs has a peak at 50 and a larger peak at 59–60. I would more broadly interpret this as demand for catered affairs peaking in the 50s. Clothing rental peaks in the early 40s with a secondary peak at 50.

I don't think this tells the entire story, however. The largest catered event that most people will ever host is a wedding. And clothing rental is generally for just two purposes—senior proms and weddings.

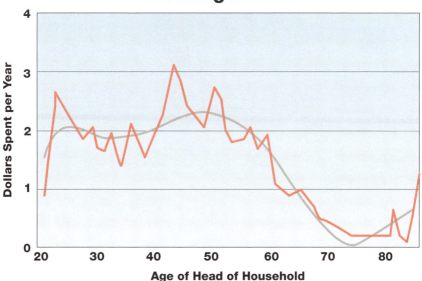

Figure 7.5

While the Boomers would appear to be in or past the peak spending age here, most still have not had the expense of their children's weddings yet. Because the Echo Boomers are getting married later on average than the generations before them, their parents, the Baby Boomers, will be taking on these expenses later in life than these charts suggest.

This is the problem with using this type of demographic analysis. Looking at the raw data is never enough. You have to take it to the next level of understanding who the ultimate beneficiary of the purchase is. If you recall, I mentioned in the introduction external economic shocks can throw off natural demographic trends by a few years, and catered affairs is a good example. But the biggest key point to remember is that the consumer life cycle ultimately revolves around kids and where they are in their development.

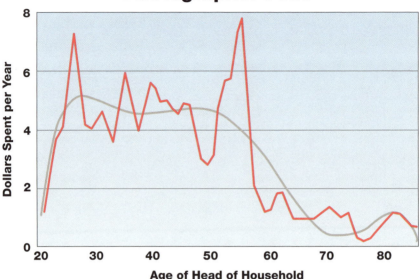

Figure 7.6

Let's also take a look at photographer fees (Figure 7.6). Photographer fees initially peak at age 26—presumably due to the cost of wedding photos—and remain fairly constant until a larger peak around 55, after which point they drop off a cliff. In the case of photographer fees, up-and-coming Echo Boomers should more than offset declining Baby Boomers. But again, if you assume that a fair bit of the photography spending by both 26-year-olds and 55-year-olds are for weddings, the demographic trends here are more favorable than we might normally expect. It's the same families making the same expenses; it's just a question of whether it is mom and dad paying the bill or the wedding couple.

The Echo Boomers are just leaving education and entering the workforce. This means that, for all of the boom in wedding planning in recent years, a much bigger boom is coming, and soon. Young people are shouldering more of the cost of their weddings than they used to, but their parents will still contribute.

Bottom line: There is a fortune to be made in all businesses related to weddings from now until roughly 2020.

Moving on, let's now take a look at demand for painting and wallpapering labor (Figure 7.7) and for contract labor and new construction (Figure 7.8). We see very different patterns here.

Demand for hardcore remodeling and new construction has an initial peak around 34 and a larger peak at 57. This is fairly intuitive; as our families grow we have increasing needs for space, which could mean making alterations to existing space or, say, building an apartment over the garage. And after our children leave the nest, we might feel like making significant changes, as we find new uses for the bedrooms and family room. But by our late 50s, we've done all of the heavy remodeling we need to do.

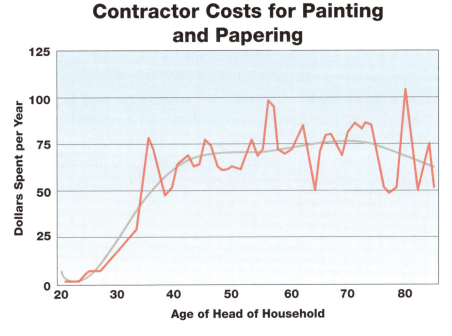

Figure 7.7

Demand for light remodeling, such as painting and wallpapering, stays fairly constant well into our 70s. There are a couple reasons for this. First, as we age we tend to spend more time in our homes, so it makes sense to invest a little money in making it an attractive place. Secondly, painting and wallpapering are relatively inexpensive projects, at least compared to tearing down walls and doing major remodeling. And finally, while we might have been willing to do the painting ourselves at an earlier stage of life, by late middle age we would prefer to pay someone else to do the grunt work.

There are a couple major points to take away from this. First, all else being equal, major remodeling will not be a good business to be in going forward. Baby Boomer spending will start declining significantly in a few years, and the Echo Boomers will not be taking up the slack any time soon.

And this would be under normal conditions, but conditions today are anything but normal. Given that the economy remains fragile and home equity loans are hard to get, I expect demand for major remodeling to be even worse than demographic trends suggest. Remember, major remodeling is expensive, and few Americans have the cash on hand to pay for it. Home equity loans were used to plug this gap over the past few decades. Plus, with the abundance of homes on the market selling at relatively cheap prices, it makes less sense to invest a lot of money in an existing structure. Why not just sell it, buy a bigger house, and avoid the headache? It's easier to get a conforming mortgage loan than to get a home equity loan.

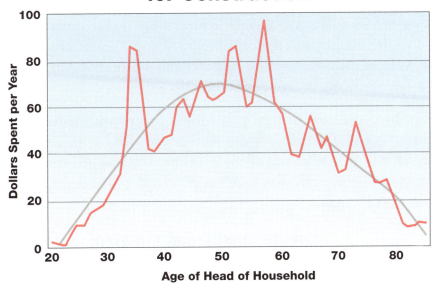

Figure 7.8

However, demographic trends for light remodeling, such as painting and papering, are excellent. The Baby Boomers have another two decades of demand in front of them, and the Echo Boomers are just starting up the steepest point of the curve. So, this is one of the few product or service areas where you stand to benefit from both the Baby Boomers and the Echo Boomers.

Furthermore, as the foreclosure logjam slowly gets broken down and housing inventory starts to make its way back to the market, there should be strong demand from current owners trying to make their homes presentable for sale and from new owners wanting to customize their home to reflect their tastes.

Bottom line: There should be excellent opportunities for skilled painters and craftsmen doing light remodeling work.

Business should also be good for the Orkin Man and his competitors. Termite and pest control (Figure 7.9) does not peak until well into our 70s. Demand for these services is inflexible; if you have a pest problem, you are going to pay to get it taken care of. Older people in older homes are likely to have more problems with pests. And while you might be tempted to spray for roaches or knock down that wasp nest yourself as a 30-year-old, the prospect of doing that is a lot less appealing at the age of 60 or 70.

So, bad economy or not, pest control businesses should have a stable and rising demand in the years ahead. And if anything, the state of disrepair of much of the enormous backlogged foreclosure inventory might mean even better opportunities than demographics alone would suggest.

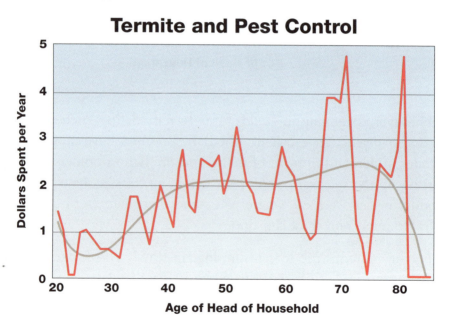

Figure 7.9

The same is not true with electrical system repair (Figure 7.10). Electrical system repair peaks at 50 and at 68 before going into a long decline. This may at first seem counterintuitive; after all, you have to pay to fix your electrical system when it breaks, no matter how old you are.

But as we age, we consume less electricity and are less taxing on our home electrical systems. We use the large appliances that use the most electricity less and have fewer electronic gadgets in the house.

So, if you are an electrician, your services will not necessarily be in decline, but you might want to broaden the services you offer. Instead of focusing solely on the electrical system, consider moving to a related area, such as installing home security systems. Or, consider using your skills to modernize older homes by installing the cabling for home networks for use with Internet-enabled TVs and other entertainment devices. With your core electrician service offering mediocre growth prospects, you will want to explore alternatives.

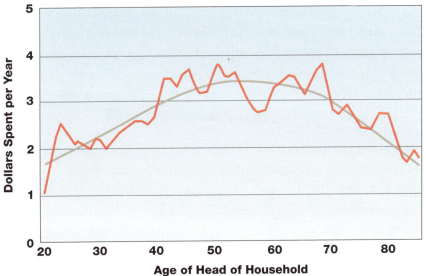

Figure 7.10

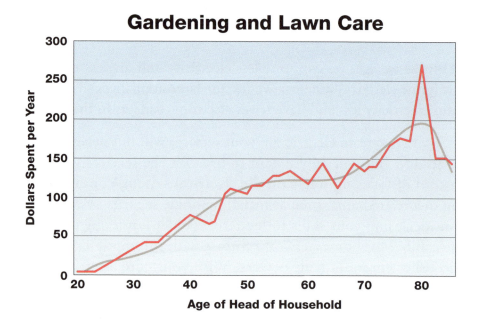

Figure 7.11

As I briefly mentioned in the section on lawn equipment, gardening and lawn care services (Figure 7.11) have strong demand based on demographics. Spending on these services rises for as long as we live in our homes. In fact, demand growth for gardening and lawn care starts to accelerate at exactly the time when overall spending starts to turn down, around the 50-year mark.

In a weak economy, some homeowners will choose to cut costs by mowing their own lawns. This is particularly true for cash-strapped young families. But the key here is that the greatest demand comes from consumers over the age of 50. So, the Baby Boomers will be an excellent source of growth in this segment for decades to come.

The next two charts are some of my favorites in the entire book because we can all relate to them on some level. Figures 7.12 and 7.13 track personal care services for women and men, respectively. These cover everything from haircuts to manicures to eyebrow waxing. It's a rough estimate of the money we spend to keep ourselves looking good.

Women never stop making the effort. Spending levels off around age 50, but continues to rise slightly until well into the 70s. Though hairstyles change, a woman cares as much about the appearance of her hair at the age of 70 as she does as a teenager, and she has more money to spend on it.

Men? Not so much. After the age of 40, most men let themselves go. If they still have their hair (the lucky ones!) they tend to spend less money taking care of it. I call Figure 7.13 the "Al Bundy" chart in honor of the main character from the 1980s' sitcom *Married with Children*. Poor Al is a working class Everyman who has largely given up on life. He feels no need to invest in his appearance. What's the point? His appearance matters little in his career, and being married with children means he is out of the dating game.

What conclusions are we to glean from this? The first and most obvious is that women are better lifelong customers for the personal care services than men. Men top out in their late 30s and it is downhill from there.

That said, with the personal care industry for women already saturated, marketing efforts have gone towards convincing younger men to invest more in their appearances. Call it the "rise of the metrosexual," but younger men today are more willing to pay up for items generally thought of as products for women, such as skin creams and high-end hair products. And this is not just in America; East Asian men, and particularly high-income Chinese men, have become a new target market in this industry, as well as in markets that are almost exclusively for women in North America—such as handbags.

So, if you own a business that caters to the personal care services of men or women—such as a hair salon—Echo Boomer men may be an area for growth over the next decade.

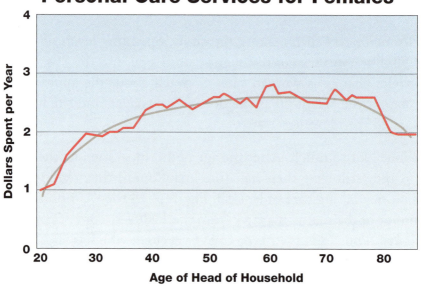

Figure 7.12

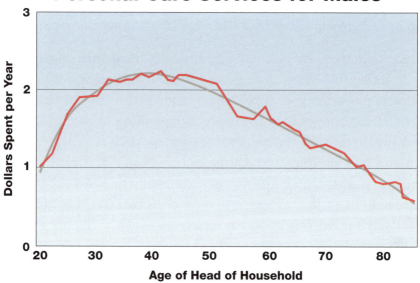

Figure 7.13

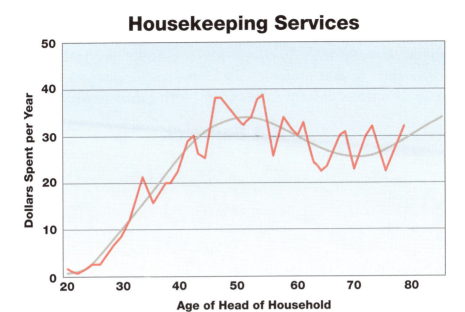

Figure 7.14

Next up is housekeeping services (Figure 7.14). Demand for housekeeping services steadily increases throughout the power working years of the 30s and 40s, though it starts to fall after the age of 54. It doesn't fall too aggressively, however, which makes sense. Once accustomed to having someone else do the chores, most Americans are not particularly eager to start again. But at the same time, with the children out of the house, there is less mess to clean and less need to spend the money on cleaning.

The takeaway here is that demand for housekeeping services should remain relatively constant in the years ahead as most Boomers will not be cutting back here. Growth, where it happens, will come from young working Echo Boomer couples. As the Echo Boomers settle into their careers, and into marriage and childrearing, their demand for housekeeping and related services will soar.

One caveat here is the overall health of the economy. If the economy remains in slow growth mode, demand for housekeeping should remain pretty healthy. But should unemployment take another major turn for the worse, then Americans who could only marginally afford to have their houses professionally cleaned will opt to clean their houses themselves or learn to be content with a dirty house!

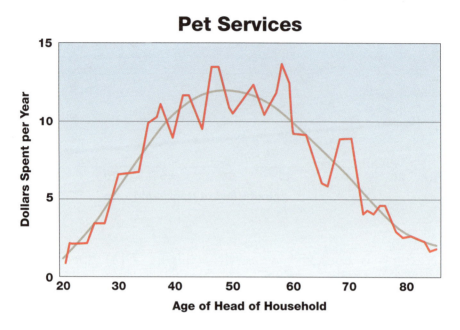

Figure 7.15

Pet services (Figure 7.15) peak at age 47 and again at 58. There are interesting implications here. Most obviously, there is some truth to the stereotype of the empty nester who buys a dog for companionship after their kids leave home.

The other takeaway is that we tend to spend quite a bit on pets and pet-related expenses for our children, but we do so when they are older. Few of us want or need the responsibility of a training a dog when we have infants or very young children in the house.

What does this mean for pet breeders and suppliers of pet-related services? Business will start to slow in the coming years and then get tougher when the Boomers pass into their 60s, a decade from now. The Echo Boomers will eventually buy puppies and kittens for their children, but the more pressing issue is that in another five years the Baby Boomers will start spending less and less.

Moving on to less glamorous topics, consider trash and garbage collection for owned homes (Figure 7.16). Our expenses here tend to rise with the size of our homes but remain constant from the late 40s on.

For most investors, this is not going to be an investable theme. Trash collection is a utility service that is typically provided by the city or municipal government. That said, there may be opportunities here if you have a way to reduce the government's costs.

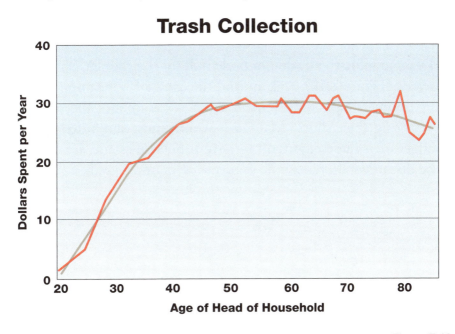

Figure 7.16

City, county, and state governments have struggled since the onset of the 2008 crisis. Falling property values and lower consumer spending meant lower revenues in property and sales taxes. Given the macro headwinds facing this country—and given the enormous pension and healthcare liabilities many local governments face for their aging workforces—there may be opportunities for privatization. Larger firms like Waste Management will be the primary beneficiaries, but a crafty entrepreneur might find a niche opportunity here, particularly in a smaller city or town that might be off the radar of a larger company.

Water softening services (Figure 7.17) have an excellent demographic profile. Demand continues to rise well into our 70s, and is particularly steep in the 20s and early 30s. This means that both the Baby Boomers and the Echo Boomers will be significant contributors to growing demand.

Furthermore, any improvement in the housing market should be a beneficial tailwind for this industry.

Demographic trends do not bode well for the cobbler. Shoe repair expenses (Figure 7.18) peak around the age of 45, meaning that the Baby Boomers have already spent the greatest amount they ever will in repairing their shoes. Making it worse, most shoes designed for younger men these days tend to have rubber soles and are designed to be discarded after a couple years rather than repaired.

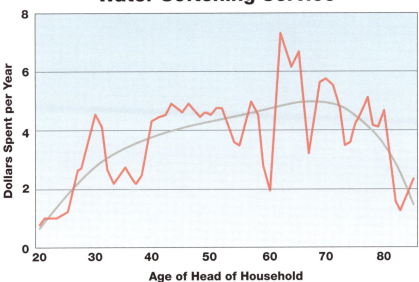

Figure 7.17

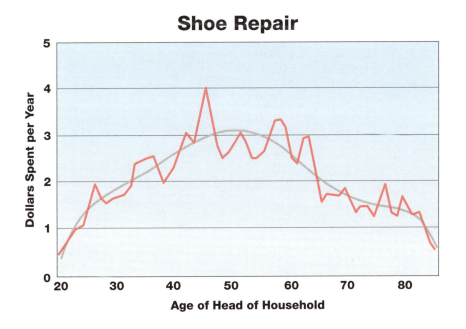

Figure 7.18

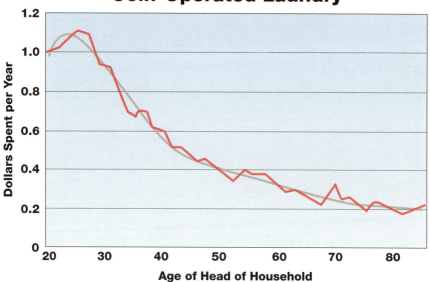

Figure 7.19

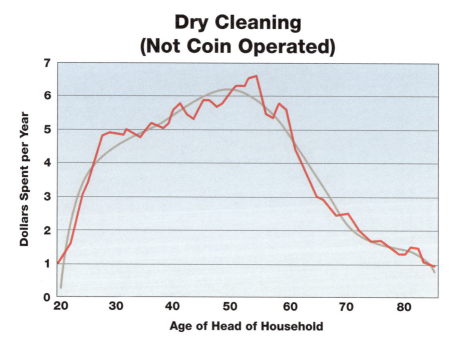

Figure 7.20

Though not as bad as coin-operated laundry (Figure 7.19), coin-operated laundromats are almost entirely a service for the young. Demand peaks by age 25 and then promptly falls off a cliff, never to recover. As the Echo Boomers grow up and climb the ladder of social respectability, they will first rent apartments with laundry appliances provided and then eventually graduate to a house of their own. This is a long way of saying that demographic trends for coin-operated laundry are severely negative.

Adding insult to injury, the large decline in immigration after the 2008 crisis took away a major low-income demographic that would be more likely to use a laundromat. Unless you own a laundromat in a neighborhood with a constant supply of college students, I would recommend staying away from this business for the foreseeable future.

Dry cleaners (Figure 7.20) are also in for a rough couple of years. Dry cleaning demand peaks just after total spending around age 54. This means that the Baby Boomers are no longer a rising market for these services.

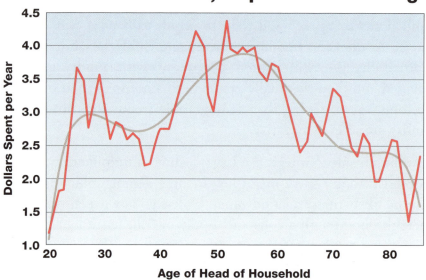

Figure 7.21

I should also note that dry cleaners are a very localized business. When you need something dry cleaned, you generally go to a cleaner within a couple miles from your house. For dry cleaners in neighborhoods dominated by Baby Boomers, this is bad news. But dry cleaners setting up shop in new neighborhoods populated with young Echo Boomer families will have a very different business climate. Spending on dry cleaning rises at a very fast rate throughout the 20s and early 30s.

So, as with real estate, the most important factors for dry cleaning success are location, location, location. If you own a dry cleaner in an older neighborhood populated mostly by Baby Boomers, consider relocating.

The same is true of tailoring (Figure 7.21). Demand for clothes tailoring peaks around the age of 51, but the takeaway is the same. The Baby Boomers are pretty much done here. If you are a tailor or seamstress, consider relocating to a neighborhood dominated by young families.

Mobile phone service (Figure 7.22) is one that I include knowing full well that my data is already obsolete. This is such a rapidly changing industry that government data will always be obsolete by the time it is published, and historical data is going to be less useful.

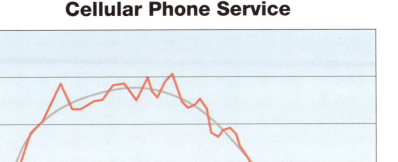

Figure 7.22

We have multiple overlapping trends here. First, older people are using cell phones more because they've grown into them. Today's 70-year-old has likely used a mobile phone for at least the past decade, if not significantly longer. But a 70-year-old 10 years ago might never have owned a cell phone, and now at the age of 80, probably still doesn't.

Another major theme is the shift from regular feature phones to smartphone, such as Apple's iPhone or the assorted phones that run Google's Android. This started with professional users and their work-issued BlackBerries, but now primarily consists of consumers.

And finally, we have the shift away from expensive contract plans by the major telecom firms such as AT&T and Verizon to cheaper prepaid plans by Metro PCS and other smaller upstarts. The shift away from contracts has opened doors to lower-income and younger consumers who might normally fail a credit check.

All of these themes overlap. Older consumers use more mobile features than prior generations, consumers across the board are embracing data plans, and prepaid plans are taking a larger share of both the voice and data markets.

I have no specific advice as to how to profit from these trends, and even if I did it might be obsolete by the time this book hits the printing presses. But I do encourage entrepreneurs to consider these trends because I believe that opportunities will arise. As an example, smaller outfits like Simple Mobile and Cricket Communications buy mobile service in bulk from T-Mobile and Sprint, respectively, and resell it to consumers as prepaid plans at a discounted price. Given the numbers of competitors in this area, I do not advocate jumping aboard. But I use it as an example of entrepreneurs finding new ways to profit from a fast-changing industry.

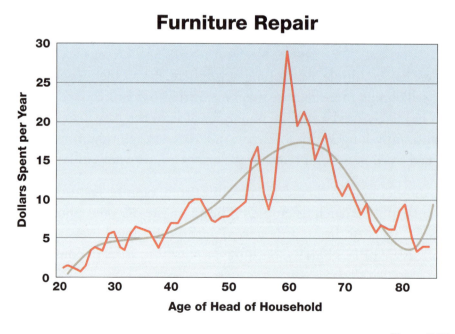

Figure 7.23

Finally, we get to furniture repair, refurnishing and reupholstery (Figure 7.23). Demand for these services peaks after the age of 60, implying that the Baby Boomers may prove to be a big source of new demand for this sleepy industry. As the empty nester Baby Boomers downsize from their large suburban homes and make major changes in their lives, some will choose to give their old furniture a facelift. This is a niche market and not a particularly easy one for an inexperienced entrepreneur to exploit. But I do expect it to do well in the years ahead.

Overall, demographic trends suggest a healthier decade ahead for consumer services relative to consumer goods. Many, though certainly not all, consumer products have demand curves that peak later in life than overall spending. I consider this area a great place to hunt for business opportunities in the 2010s.

This page intentionally left blank.

Auto and Transportation

Auto and Transportation

Autos and transportation are a critical sector of the U.S. economy. Though vehicles and vehicle parts only make up 3% of total U.S. GDP,[14] a car or truck payment is often the largest expense for an American family after their home mortgage or rent. And the auxiliary industries that make auto ownership possible—everything from financing to insurance to oil changes—employ millions. Finally, because vehicles are often purchased on credit, they tend to have an outsized impact on consumption by pulling future purchases into the present. In the circular world of economics, this means that auto sales both create economic volatility and are uniquely susceptible to its effects.

The past few years have not been kind to the auto industry. General Motors and Chrysler both had to run to the government for bailouts, and Ford only barely escaped the same fate. Annual industry sales fell from an annualized rate of 20 million units per year in July of 2005 to barely 9 million in September of 2009.[15] And the sales that did happen were often only made possible by generous incentives and financing. In a bad economy, the auto industry is not a pleasant place to be.

And it gets worse. While the automobile has been an essential part of American life for nearly a century, younger Americans appear to put a much lower priority on car ownership than previous generations. Nearly half of Echo Boomers say the Internet is more important to them than a car,[16] and fewer young people are bothering to get licenses at all. According to a recent study, 69% of 17-year-olds had a driver's license in 1983. By 2008, that number had dropped to 50%. Among Americans aged 20 to 24 nearly 92% had driver's licenses in 1983. Today it is 82% and falling.[17]

A bad economy is partially responsible for the recent drop, but it doesn't explain the long-term secular trend. There are several factors that have contributed. First, American cities are re-urbanizing, as I noted in Chapter 2. Public transit is more viable in urban cores than in sprawling suburbs. The Internet and mobile connectivity has helped too, and younger people can do more, be it for work or fun, without leaving their homes. And the bad news for automakers is that all of these trends look to continue.

Echo Boomers may be trendy urban metrosexuals at this stage of their lives, but they will not be able to escape suburbia and its minivans forever. As the Echo Boomers form families, they will drive more miles and will require more and larger cars. Such is the life of carpools and soccer practice.

Still, this won't happen tomorrow. And in the meantime, the auto industry looks to have several rough years in front of it. So, with this said, let's jump deeper into the world of automobiles and see what the demographic trends tell us.

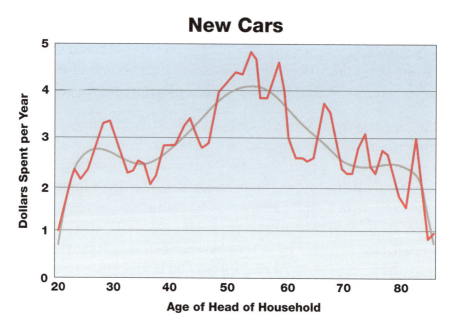

Figure 8.1

We'll start with new car sales (Figure 8.1) given their importance to the entire industry. Here, the news is not encouraging for the likes of General Motors or Ford. Spending peaks around age 53, or by 2014 for the Baby Boomers. Men or women in their late 40s and early 50s are at the peak of their career and earning power without most of the cost of raising kids anymore. Having a high-priced car is part of maintaining an image, and at 40 or 50 many of us can afford the luxury car we couldn't afford at 20 or 30.

Once the kids have left the nest, people drive much fewer miles and their cars last much longer. Hence, after 2014, it is curtains for the auto industry. Demand for the most profitable cars (i.e., luxury and high-end sports cars) will be in decline, and lower-end models for younger Echo Boomers will become more the focus. New car sales have been depressed for years due to the severity of the 2008 meltdown and the Great Recession that followed. We may get some "catch up" buying in the years ahead as American drivers replace their aging existing cars with the vehicles they would have bought years ago under better economic conditions. Again, as I said before, economic conditions can cause demographic trends to be off by a year or so. The average length of service of the cars currently on American roads is an almost unbelievable 11 years.

To some extent, automakers are being punished for their virtues in that the quality improvements of the past two decades mean that we need to replace our cars less frequently. But the trends I discussed at the beginning of this chapter are having an effect, too. Americans are driving fewer miles as city planning and development favors shorter commutes and more public transit, at least in major metro areas. The Internet makes many car trips unnecessary. And young people simply do not value car ownership the way they used to. "As needed" car sharing and rental services such as Zipcar are rising in popularity, particularly among college students and recent graduates living in urban areas.

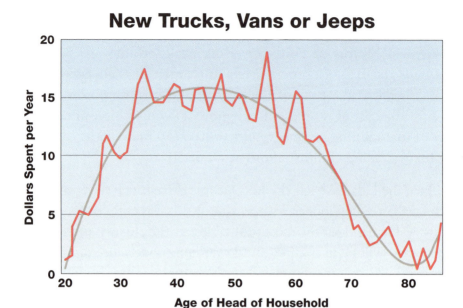

Figure 8.2

Again, the Echo Boomers will eventually grow up and buy cars. But if their youth is any indication, they may buy fewer cars as a household than their parents did. A husband and wife may opt to share a car rather than buy two. Most middle-class families in suburban or exurban areas will still need two or more cars. But in economics, it is what happens at the margin that matters. And at the margin, Echo Boomers will buy fewer cars per capita than their parents.

In looking at demand for new trucks, pick-ups, vans and Jeeps (Figure 8.2), we see a slightly different demand profile. Demand peaks earlier, around the age of 34, and levels off before having one last spike around 55.

This is an important segment of the new vehicle market. The two best-selling vehicles in the United States are the Ford F-Series and the Chevrolet Silverado pick-ups. The Dodge Ram pick-up is also in the top 10. So, weakness here will be felt.

The heyday of the large, gas-guzzling SUV has passed, due most obviously to the high price of gasoline. But demographic trends have played a big role here as well. Baby Boomer mothers no longer need or want a full-sized Suburban or Tahoe once their kids leave the nest. And minivans? Most are happy to close that chapter of their lives as soon as they possibly can.

Small and mid-sized SUVs remain very popular, however, and currently account for nearly one-third of all vehicle sales. It is debatable whether these should be classified as "trucks" given that many are built on car frames and are essentially station wagons with a higher ground clearance.

Using the historical data, it would be tempting to draw the conclusion that trucks, pick-ups, vans, and Jeeps have a brighter demographic future in front of them than cars, and this may end up being true to some extent, particularly with the Echo Boomers entering the family formation stage in the years to come. But the hard reality is that lower spending by Baby Boomers will make life very difficult for the entire industry. And the Echo Boomers will not have the impact that the Baby Boomers did when their peak spending years eventually arrive.

Bottom line: The auto industry cannot expect a sustained recovery for at least a decade, and when that recovery comes it will be less impressive than those of decades past. I would not advise owning a car dealership or getting involved in this industry.

The demographic profiles of the used vehicle market are very different. Used vehicles are more popular among younger consumers and fit better into their budgets. Used car expenditures (Figure 8.3) initially peak around the age of 23, though they have later peaks at 46 and 55. After that point, demand goes into a steep decline.

Demand for used trucks and vans (Figure 8.4) has a later initial peak, at 34, but then turns down sharply after this without the rebound in the 40s and 50s.

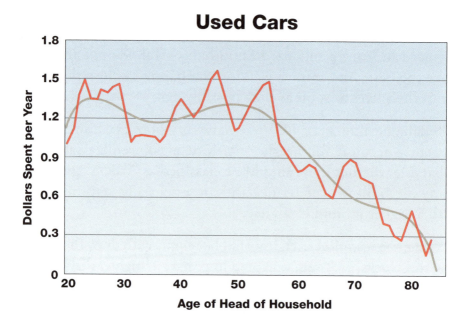

Figure 8.3

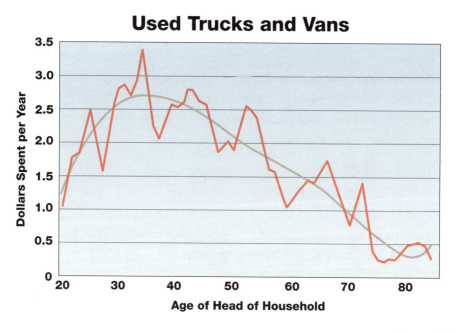

Figure 8.4

The used vehicle market is actually far more complicated to understand than the new vehicle market. New car demand is essentially driven by two factors: demographics and the health of the economy. Other factors, such as high oil prices, might affect which vehicles are purchased and how much money is spent on those vehicles, but demographic and macroeconomic forces dominate overall sales.

These same factors affect used vehicle demand, but it is also complicated more by supply factors. Fewer new vehicles sold means a smaller inventory of used cars in the years that follow, which, all else being equal, narrows the price differential between new vehicles and used vehicles. As with any commodity, limited supply causes prices to rise, and excess supply causes prices to fall. And this price differential in turn affects demand for used vehicles vis-à-vis new ones.

It's a remarkably circular and complex market dynamic. And what does it all mean going forward? Given the production cuts of recent years, I expect used car pricing to be strong for the next several years. But how are we to act on this information?

Starting or investing in a used car lot is a possibility, but the pricing cuts both ways here. The sales price will be high, but so will be your inventory cost. Still, given that cars have longer lives than ever before and that the economy will remain weak for years to come, running a used car lot would seem a better business opportunity than owning a new vehicle dealership, and your start-up costs would be a fraction of a new car dealership.

In your personal life, if you are considering buying a car, you may find that buying a new car makes sense, depending on the model in question. And if you have a late-model car in your garage that you use infrequently, you might find it makes sense to sell it.

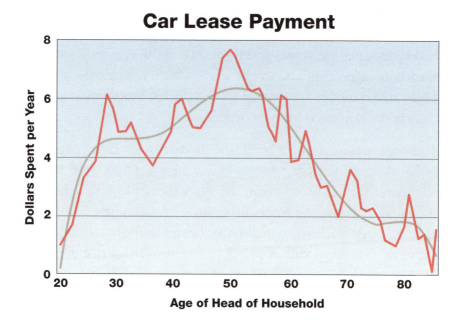

Figure 8.5

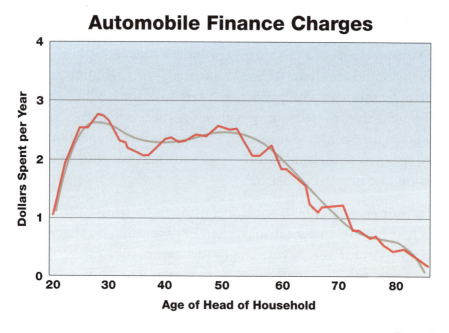

Figure 8.6

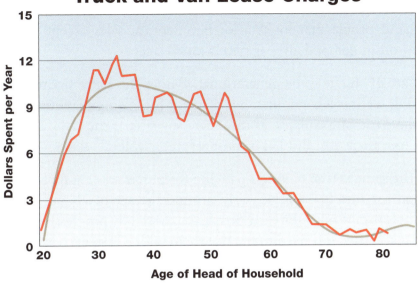

Figure 8.7

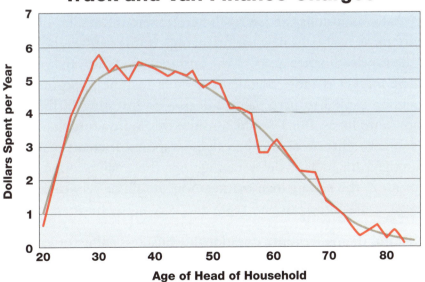

Figure 8.8

Moving into the world of auto finance, we see numbers that more or less correspond to sales. Car lease payments (Figure 8.5) have a demand profile that looks a lot like new car sales except that the drop-off in demand after age 50 is much steeper.

Part of this may be generational. Before the Baby Boomers, car leasing was far less popular. So, demand for leasing may not exhibit as dramatic of a collapse as this chart suggests as the Baby Boomers age into their 50s. But fall it most assuredly will.

The same is true of auto financing for purchases (Figure 8.6). Demand for auto loans peaks early, around the age of 28 and remains fairly constant until the early 50s. Though we buy progressively more expensive cars, our need to finance them with a loan decreases as our incomes rise.

Truck and van leasing and finance charges (Figures 8.7 and 8.8) both peak in the early 30s before turning down sharply. Truck and van leasing peaks at 33, whereas finance charges peak at 30.

What conclusions can we reach here? There is not a lot of opportunity for investors in new car financing, as this tends to be covered by the captive finance arms of the automakers. Given that the used vehicle market is more fragmented, there may be opportunities in providing capital to used vehicle dealers or investing in funds that supply auto loans. But I would consider this more a function of capital market tightness rather than demographics. If credit markets remain tight due to bank deleveraging, then there will be opportunities to profit in the private loan market. You should be very careful here, however, as lending can be a risky, and very messy business.

If autos themselves are a questionable business going forward, then what about the auxiliary industries that support them?

The market for vehicle insurance (Figure 8.9) looks weak. Demand peaks at age 50 and then goes into steep decline. This means that the

Baby Boomers are largely finished here, and for the reasons I discussed earlier we can't expect a large boost from the Echo Boomers. If you sell auto insurance, you should consider moving your practice to a different product area.

Auto repair service policies (Figure 8.10) and membership fees for auto service clubs (Figure 8.11) are two areas that should continue to see growth, however. This area is concentrated in dealer-sold policies and in large third-party sellers such as AAA, but if you have connections and expertise in the auto industry, then you may want to explore ways to profit from this trend. It is one of the few ways I see to profit from the auto industry in the foreseeable future.

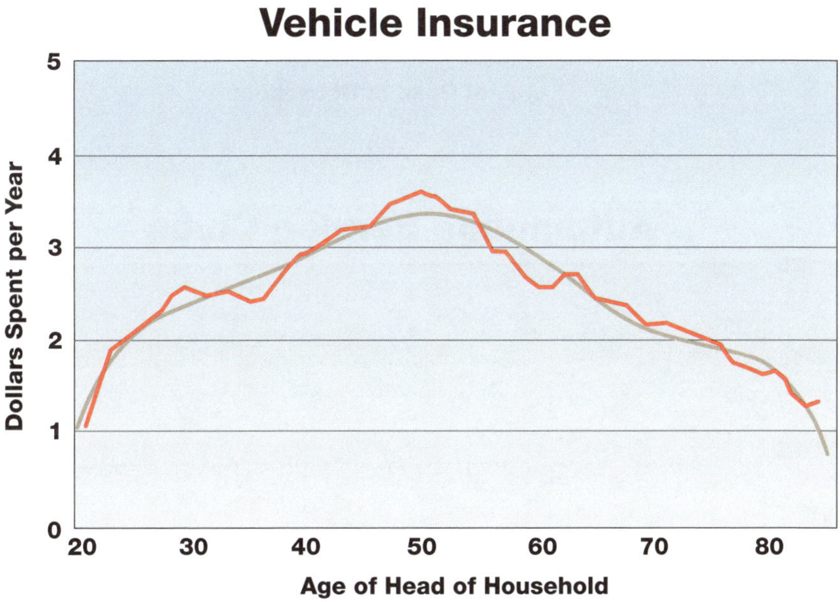

Vehicle Insurance

Figure 8.9

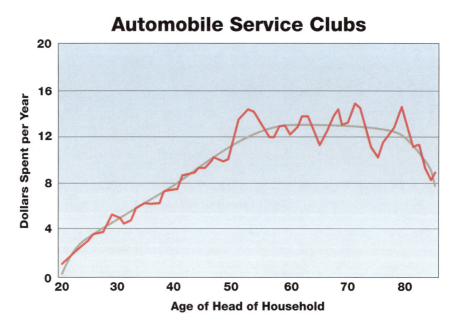

Figure 8.10

Figure 8.11

144

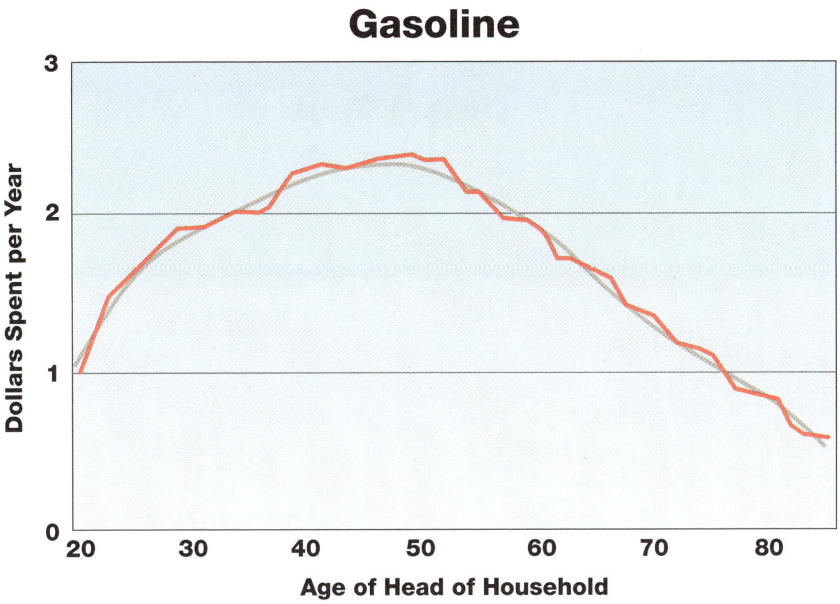

Gasoline

[Figure: Line chart titled "Gasoline" showing Dollars Spent per Year (0 to 3) vs Age of Head of Household (20 to 80+). Curve rises from ~1 at age 20, peaks around 2.3 near age 50, then declines to ~0.6 by age 85.]

Figure 8.12

Gasoline consumption (Figure 8.12) peaks around 50, as does diesel fuel (figure 8.13). Motor oil (Figure 8.14) peaks at 43. Demand for oil and lube changes as a service (Figure 8.15) peaks later, at age 56, but in all four cases the Baby Boomers have already largely had the biggest impact they are ever going to, and we can't expect much of a boost from the Echo Boomers.

As we age, we drive less. Our lives, though still vibrant, simply require less driving than they used to. This is made worse by a sagging economy, which has kept unemployment high and retail activity low, and by the rise of Internet commerce.

Less driving means lower fuel consumption, which means less traffic for gas stations. But there are also knock-on effects. Gas stations earn most of their profits from the convenience stores inside that sell everything from cigarettes and beer, to lunchmeat and juice. Lower traffic to the gas stations also means fewer convenience store purchases. And the movement towards more fuel-efficient vehicles doesn't help either. A Toyota Prius hybrid requires fewer pit stops than a Ford F-150.

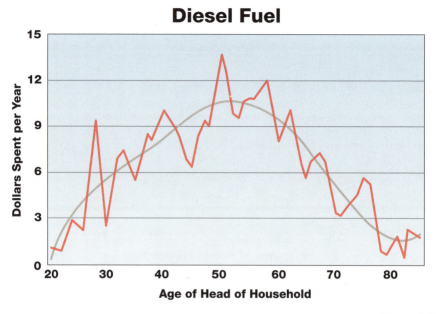

Figure 8.13

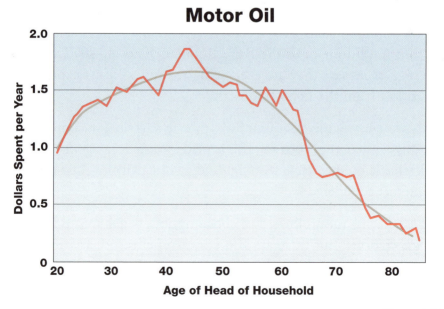

Figure 8.14

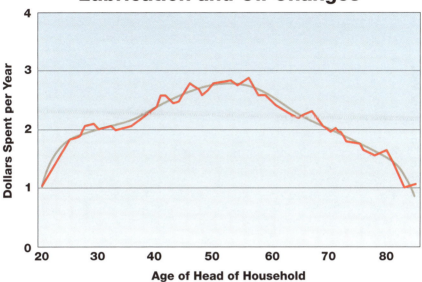

Figure 8.15

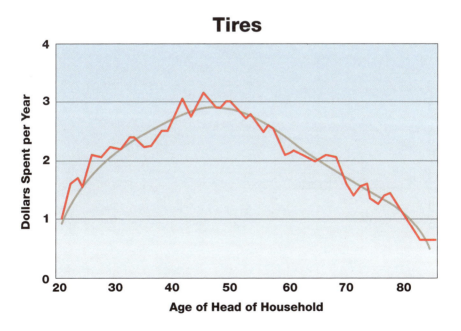

Figure 8.16

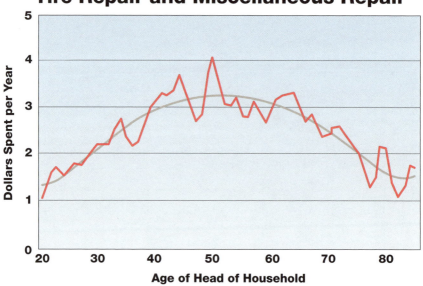

Figure 8.17

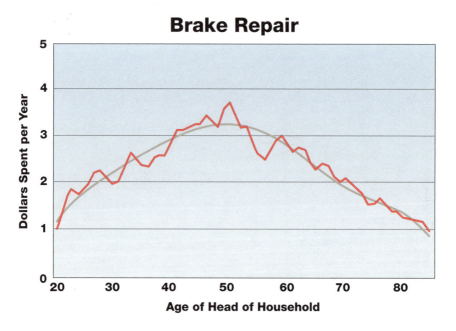

Figure 8.18

Less driving also means less need for basic maintenance and replacement parts like tires (Figure 8.16), tire repair (Figure 8.17), brake work (Figure 8.18), clutch and transmission repair (Figure 8.19), motor repair and replacement (Figure 8.20), and motor tune-ups (Figure 8.21), all of which peak in spending within a few years of age 50. The only potential saving grace here is that the tendency of Americans to own their cars for longer periods of time might partially mitigate the natural demographic-based declines. But again, this would be a partial mitigation at best.

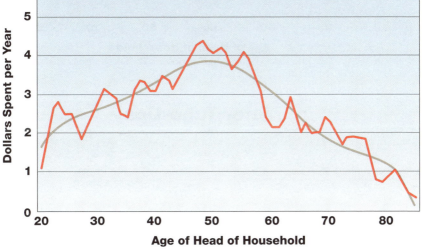

Figure 8.19

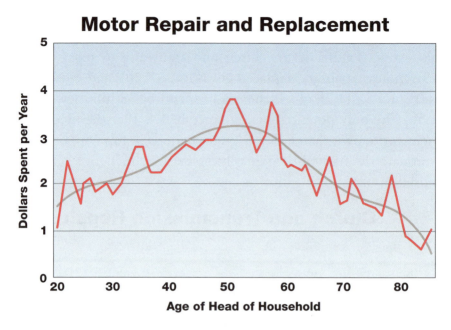

Figure 8.20

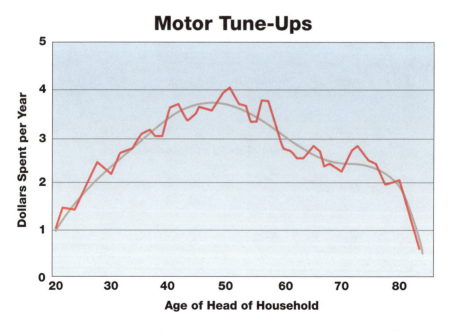

Figure 8.21

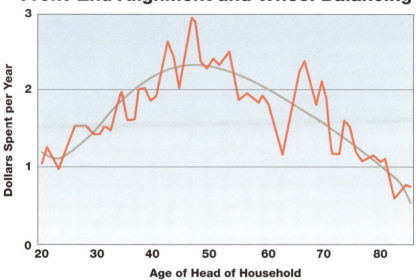

Figure 8.22

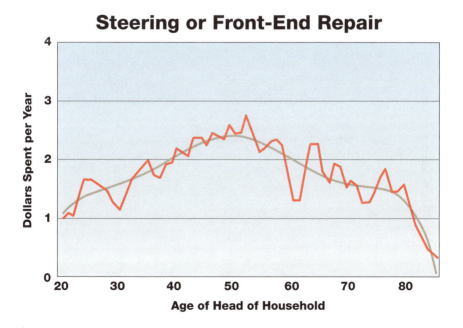

Figure 8.23

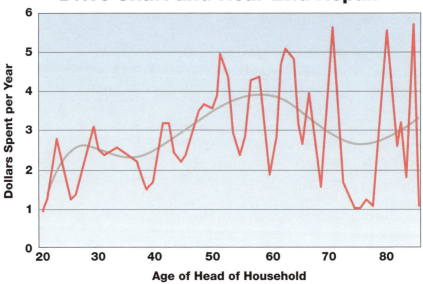

Figure 8.24

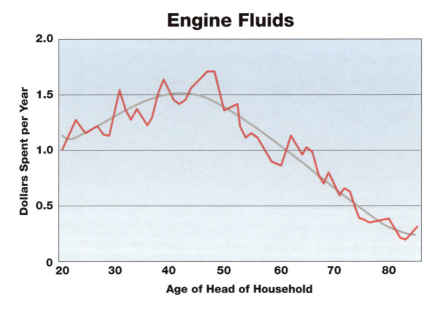

Figure 8.25

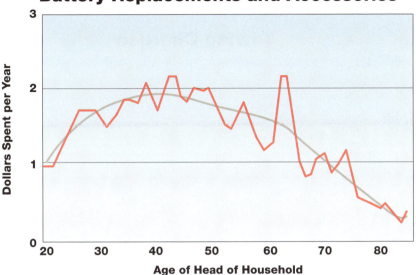

Figure 8.26

The situation for front-end alignment, wheel balancing, tire rotation (Figure 8.22) and steering or front end repair (Figure 8.23) also peak in the late 40s or early 50s, though drive shaft and rear-end repair (Figure 8.24) has an erratic pattern due to data thinness. Front-end alignment peaks at age 46, steering and front-end repair peaks at age 52, and drive shaft and rear-end repair peaks at 51 before the data gets erratic.

Coolant and other fluids (Figure 8.25) peak at 47. Battery replacement, floor mats, filters and other assorted parts (Figure 8.26) peaks at 42–43 and then has a late spike in the early 60s. It's hard to see much of an investable theme here, however.

Even tow truck drivers have a rough demographic picture in front of them (Figure 8.27). Demand for towing services is high when we first start driving and remains relatively constant until dropping like a rock after the age of 50. Less driving means less demand for towing services. Some of the decline is masked by service club memberships such as AAA, however. The driver will oftentimes not pay for the towing charges directly but will instead pay via AAA.

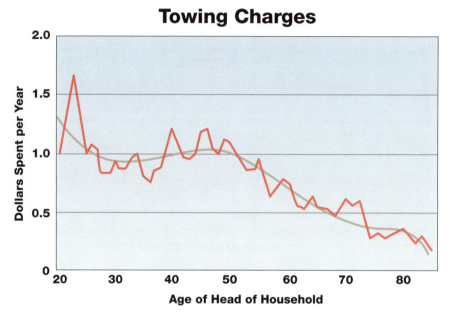

Figure 8.27

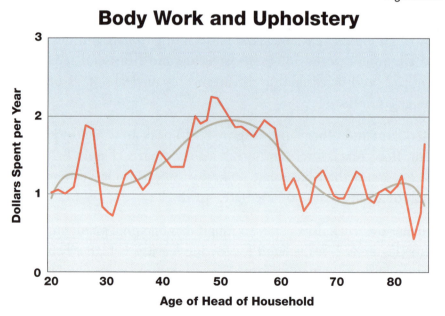

Figure 8.28

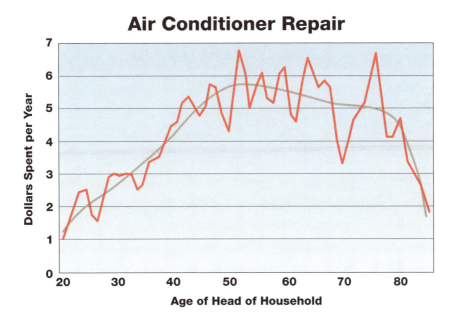

Figure 8.29

Nor do demographics point to a bright future for body and paint shops. Demand for body work, upholstery, painting and assorted repairs (Figure 8.28) peaks around age 49.

Interestingly, demand for air conditioning repair (Figure 8.29) stays relatively stable after peaking around the age of 51. It appears that the older we get, the less willing we are to swelter in our cars, even if we spend less time driving!

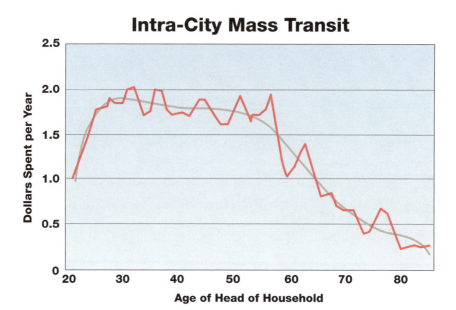

Figure 8.30

If you glean anything from this chapter, let it be this: The auto industry and all of its complementary sub-industries are in for difficult times in the years ahead. This is an industry that is heavily dependent on the health of the economy, and even the most optimistic of economists stop short of forecasting strong growth over the next decade. In the best case scenario, we may have modest growth, and in the worst case scenario we could actually see significant shrinkage.

But even in a normal economic environment, demographic trends point to a bleak future, and not just for auto sales. Even demand for bus and taxi services (Figures 8.30 and 8.31) will fall as Baby Boomers scale back. Demand for buses falls dramatically after 56, and demand for taxis starts to trend downward after 54.

If your business revolves around the auto industry, you have serious choices to make. If you have the flexibility to sell your business, you may want to consider doing so. If this is not a realistic option, then prepare to compete by perhaps offering greater specialization, customization, or focusing on a niche market.

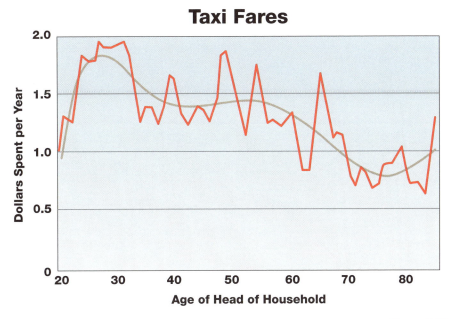

Figure 8.31

And for the next several years, focus on cutting costs and reducing your overhead wherever possible. Some years will be better than others, but the overall trend for the foreseeable future will be one of slow growth or shrinkage.

This page intentionally left blank.

Children's Goods and Services

Children's Goods and Services

I have breaking news for you: Kids cost money! As I outlined in the introduction, kids cost parents a shocking amount of money — as in hundreds and hundreds of thousands of dollars. They come into this world as a major expense, and they get continually more expensive until they move out of the house. And if you are paying for their university education, then the expenses get ratcheted up to a whole new level.

More than just increasing the amount of money we spend, children change the way we spend it. Rather than focus our consumption on ourselves, our disposable dollars go to pay for the wants and needs of our children — everything from Mickey Mouse dolls to bunk beds.

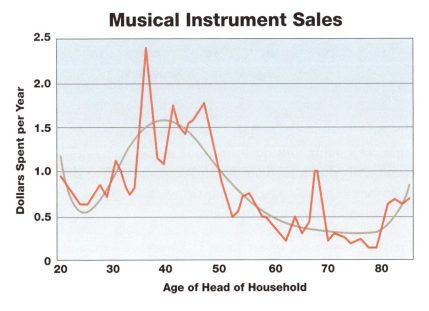

Figure 9.1

Let's start with musical instrument sales, and music instrument rentals and repairs (Figures 9.1 and 9.2). Spending peaks at 36 and

40, respectively. Might some of this be 30-something men having an early mid-life crisis and starting a garage band? I suppose. But it is safe to say that the overwhelming majority of these expenses are for school-aged children joining their school band.

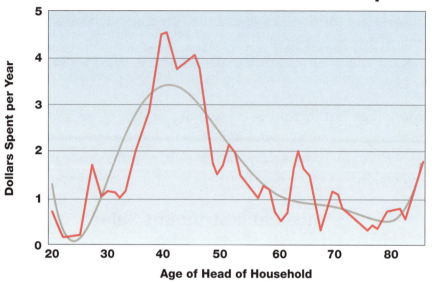

Figure 9.2

The Baby Boomers passed this stage a full decade ago, so the damage that their aging will do to musical instrument sales has already been done. In the immediate future, demand will be driven by the children born in the years leading up to 2007, what is tentatively called "Generation Z" in the press.

The largest number of births in U.S. history happened in 2007, even bigger than the peak years of the original 1950s' and 1960s' baby boom (although when adjusted for immigration, the peak years of the original baby boom are still bigger).

Most children pick up a musical instrument around the age of 11 or 12. So, I would expect demand for "starter" musical instruments to get progressively stronger from now until 2018–2019. And on a 3–4-year lag, I would expect a boom in higher-end "professional class" instruments.

The dollar signs here will shock parents who have never played an instrument. The cost of a typical Selmer alto saxophone will often run well over $5,000, and you might have to mortgage your house if your child takes to the tuba or cello. Professional caliber instruments such as these can be more expensive than a car.

But beyond the instruments themselves, there are the supporting industries such as private lessons. Parents will spend $20 for a half hour lesson, and more for the most sought-after instructors.

This is not a business opportunity that just anyone can participate in. Professional expertise and connoisseurship are required. But for those of you with the skills and knowledge, there should be opportunities in all businesses related to musical instruments.

Further down the line, a much larger boom will come when the Echo Boomers hit their late 30s and early 40s. But that will be the late 2020s. The boom that I am speaking of can be thought of as more of a "mini boom" from the children of Generation X.

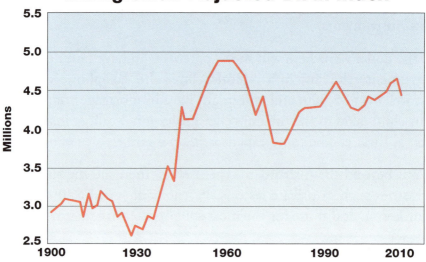

Figure 9.3

Let's step back for a moment to review the Immigration-Adjusted Birth Index (Figure 9.3). The largest demographic force in America remains the Baby Boomers, as you can very easily see by the large bulge in the middle of the graph. Not only were births in the United States at record highs in the late 1950s and early 1960s, but immigrants in the 1970s, '80s and early '90s swelled their ranks even further.

As the vast majority of Baby Boomers are now empty nesters or have adult kids in the home, this generation will not be much of a factor in this chapter. The key generations to watch for children's goods and services will be the Echo Boomers, who saw their peak birth year in 1990, and Generation Z, who saw their peak birth year in 2007. The front end of the Echo Boomers is already settling into family life, but most of the births in Generation Z are to Generation X mothers. Generation X, in case you need a refresher, is the "Baby Bust" generation wedged between the Baby Boomers and the Echo Boomers.

If I have succeeded in confusing you, let me put it to you like this: There was a large generation of kids born leading up to 2007, so this mini-boom can be thought of as a wave that will push through the economy in the years to come.

But the much larger wave is still to come. The first wave of Echo Boomers should be having more children through 2019, but the difficult economy is working against that and births are edging down instead. The next strong birth surge should occur when the second wave is rising and the economy is growing again. That will be from around 2027 to around 2036, although pent up desires for kids from the first wave could start to resurface earlier when the economy picks up around 2023 forward. The U.S. birth rate, measured as the number of babies born per 1,000 women of childbearing age, hit an all-time low in 2012, so it may take another 10-13 years for this baby bust to work its way through the system.

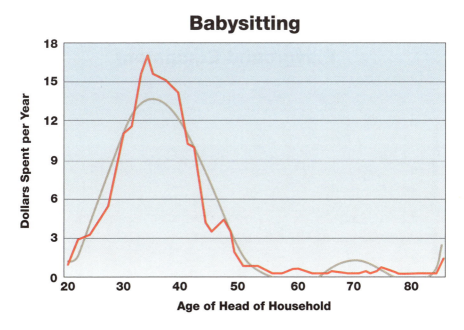

Figure 9.4

With that said, let's jump back into demographic forecasting. Demand for paid babysitting (Figure 9.4) is concentrated in the mid-30s and peaks around 34 just as the average kid born at age 28–29 is entering elementary school. The real boom in babysitting is still a few years away. But the surge in births leading up to 2007 means that demand should still be quite high in the interim.

I don't know that there is much in the way of a business opportunity here, but retiring Baby Boomers may find that watching their neighbors' children is an easy source of supplemental income. And forward-looking entrepreneurs could use the next several years as a testing period for a babysitting or nanny service with the understanding that the real money will be made in the late 2010s and 2020s when the next great baby boom gets underway.

Playground equipment (Figure 9.5) peaks at 30–31, just as children are getting old enough to crawl and jump on it. This peak is in line with starter home purchases.

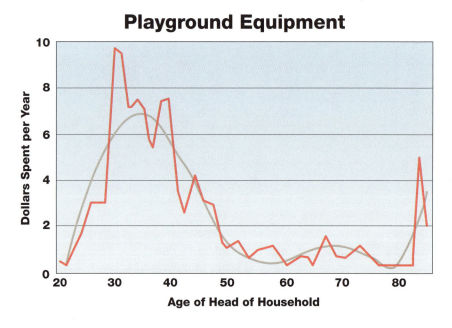

Figure 9.5

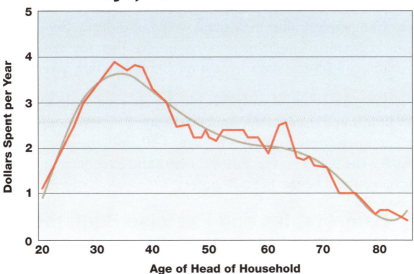

Figure 9.6

It may be a little late to take advantage of the Generation Z birth surge. The kids born in 2007 are already six years old today. But it would make sense to put the pieces in place today in order to take advantage of the next boom. Opportunities here could include designing high-end playgrounds for the kids of upper-middle-class Echo Boomer parents. Or, offering to assemble playgrounds for dads without the tools or knowhow could be an option for those with basic carpentry skills.

The same logic applies to toys, games, hobbies, tricycles and battery-powered riders (Figure 9.6). Spending here peaks at age 33 just before their children enter elementary school. I expect this age to rise going forward as the average age at first childbirth continues to rise for women. But the basic reasoning is the same: Babies born when you are in your late 20s want toys by the time you are in your early to mid-30s.

Though the demographics are straightforward, profiting from this trend may not be particularly easy. If you are trying to sell toys, you have to compete with the likes of Target, Wal-Mart and Toys R Us, among others. Competing against these titans would be difficult. But if you are looking at potential employment opportunities, then toy marketing or the making of high-end specialty toys might not be a bad career choice.

Breaking the trend of early 30s buying are Ping-Pong tables and other health and exercise equipment (Figure 9.7). Spending in this segment doesn't peak until after the age of 40. Still, the point remains the same. The Baby Boomers are done here and have been for a while. Your market will be the Echo Boomers.

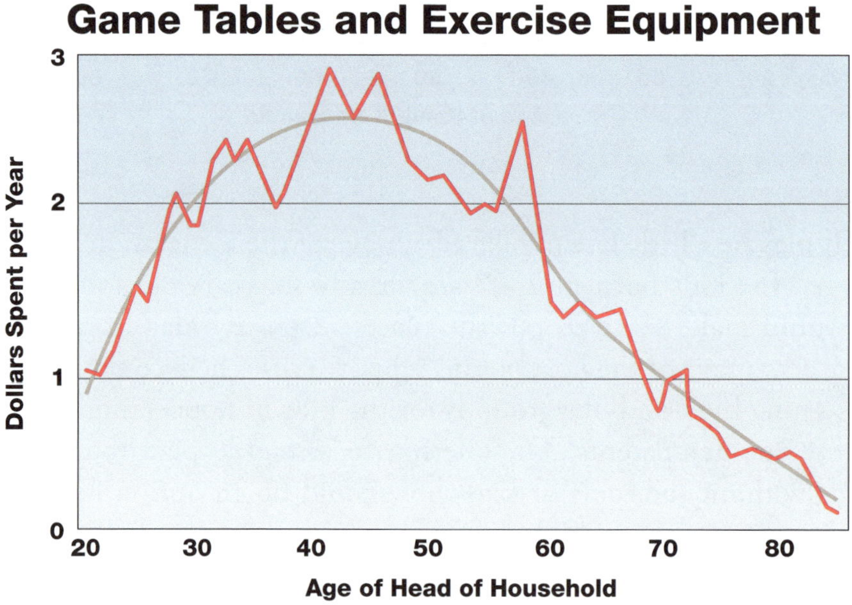

Game Tables and Exercise Equipment

Figure 9.7

The next several graphs of demand for infant products all essentially tell the same story. Demand generally peaks in the late 20s or very early 30s, in line with first childbirth. The first child is far more of an economic event than his or her subsequent siblings. It's with the first child that you have to buy the most expensive things, such as equipment (Figure 9.8) and furniture (Figure 9.9). Equipment includes such things as strollers and baby swings, and furniture includes the biggest items like the crib, dresser, changing table, etc.

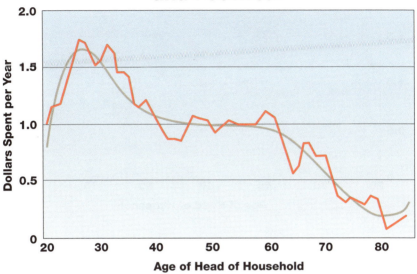

Figure 9.8

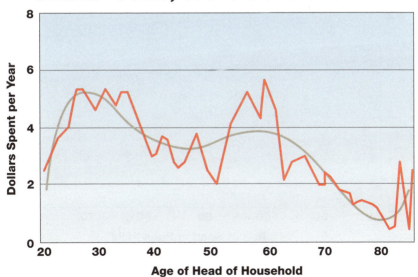

Figure 9.9

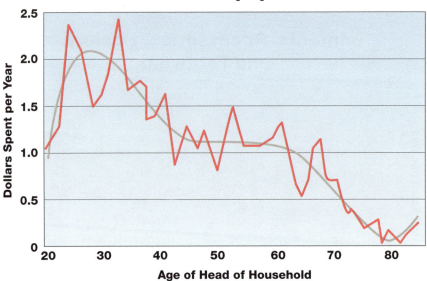

Figure 9.10

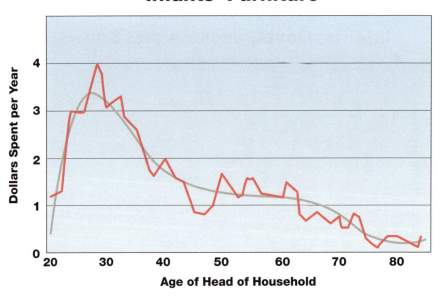

Figure 9.11

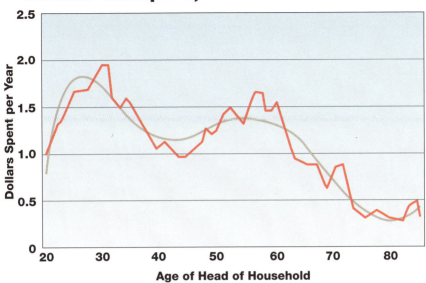

Figure 9.12

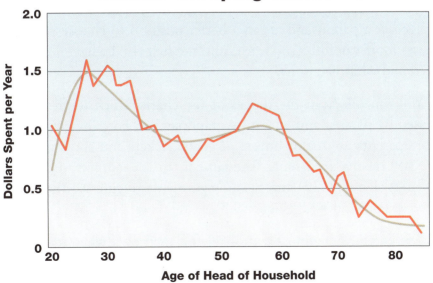

Figure 9.13

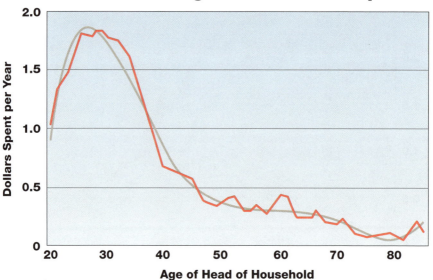

Figure 9.14

After the first child, you already own all of these things and have no need to buy it all again. But beyond this, you are also more experienced as a parent and are in a better position to choose your purchases more carefully. You learn from the first child what you actually need and what you don't.

You can tell from the shapes of the charts which items are purchased by parents and which by grandparents. For whatever reason, grandparents are major buyers of coats, jackets and snowsuits (Figure 9.9) relative to parents. The same is true of rompers, dresses and sweaters (Figure 9.12) and sleeping garments (Figure 9.13) and, to a lesser extent, footwear (Figure 9.8).

Yet, parents are almost completely on their own when it comes to buying diapers (Figure 9.14).

As I have stressed repeatedly, there is another major baby boom coming towards the end of this decade. In looking at the average 20-something Echo Boomer serving you at Starbucks, it's hard to imagine them as a mother or father. But they have a lot of growing up to do over the course of the next few years.

So, while baby products may have several uninspiring years in front of them, a boom is eventually coming. Use the next several years to position yourself accordingly.

In looking at these demand curves, you get a decent idea of who your market is. The primary buyers are the parents, and though the data doesn't give the data segregated by sex, it is safe to assume that the mother is the primary decision maker on these purchases. But for plenty of these products, grandparents are significant buyers as well. And what appeals to a baby's mother may be very different than what appeals to a baby's grandmother.

In other words, tailor your products to the tastes of Echo Boomer mothers, but don't neglect Baby Boomer grandmothers.

Large retailers tend to dominate the baby products markets. But this is an area where word-of-mouth recommendations also carry a lot of weight. If you have a concept for a new baby product, use the next several years to build your brand and develop a presence on the web and via social media. Participate in message board discussions and in the comments sections of sites and blogs that are popular with new moms. This is still wide-open territory, and the possibilities in the next boom are limitless.

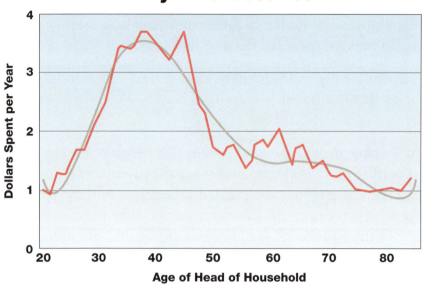

Figure 9.15

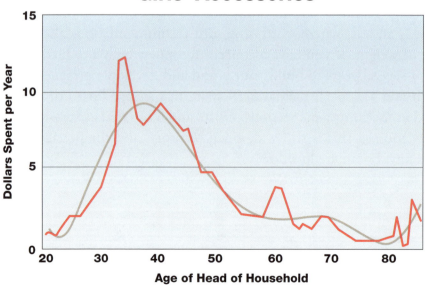

Figure 9.16

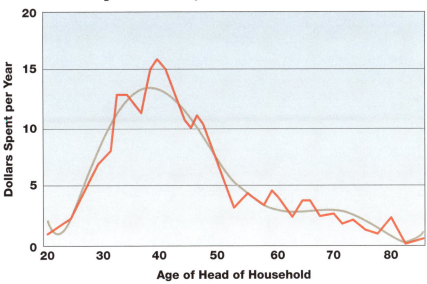

Figure 9.17

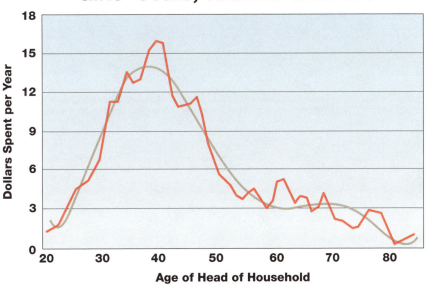

Figure 9.18

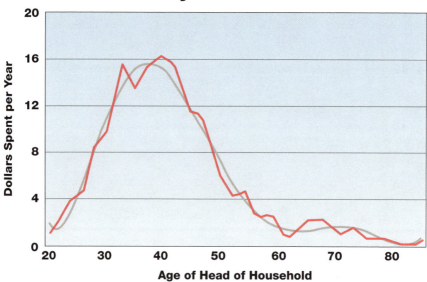

Figure 9.19

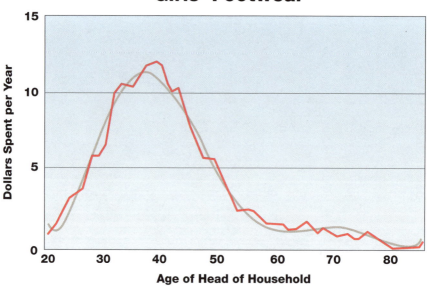

Figure 9.20

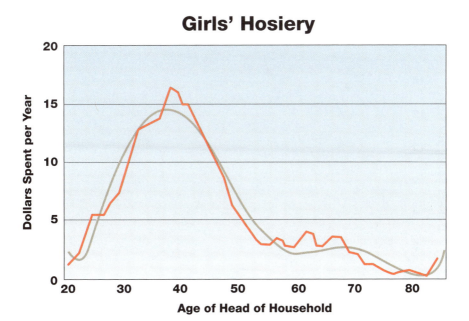

Figure 9.21

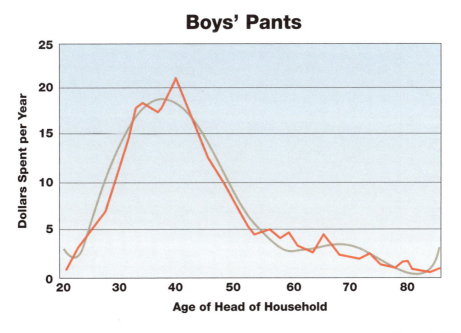

Figure 9.22

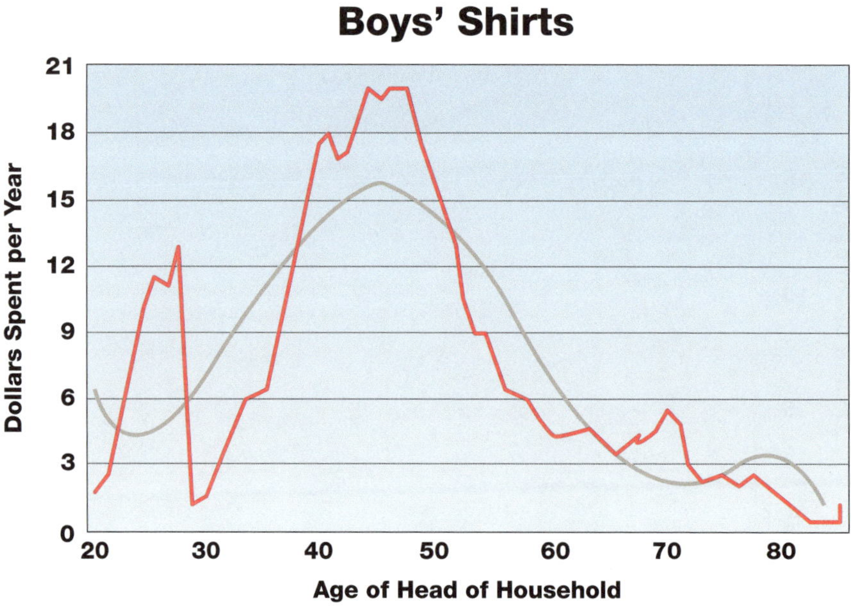

Boys' Shirts

Figure 9.23

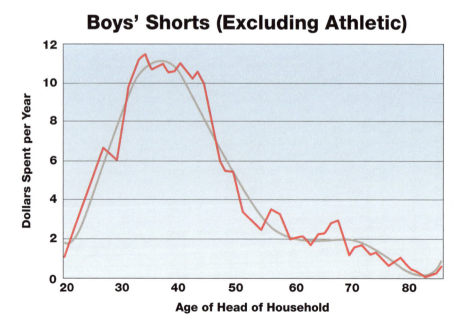

Figure 9.24

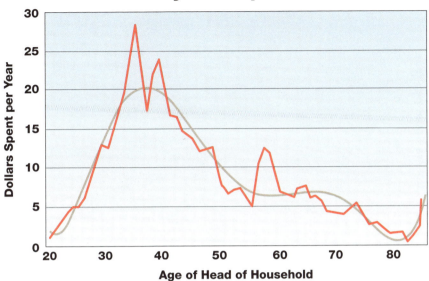

Figure 9.25

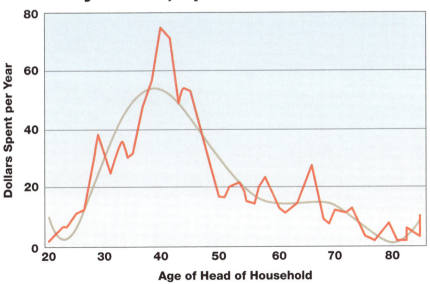

Figure 9.26

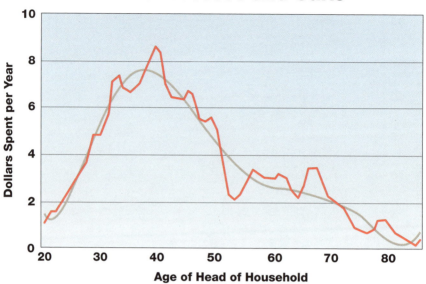

Figure 9.27

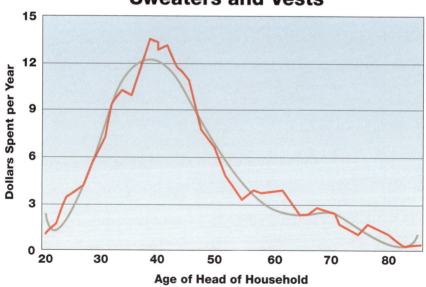

Figure 9.28

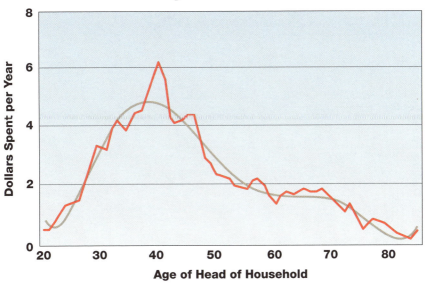

Figure 9.29

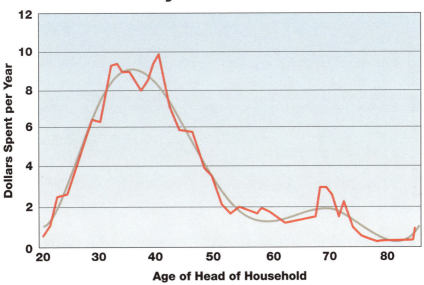

Figure 9.30

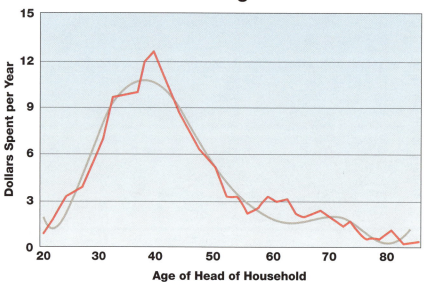

Figure 9.31

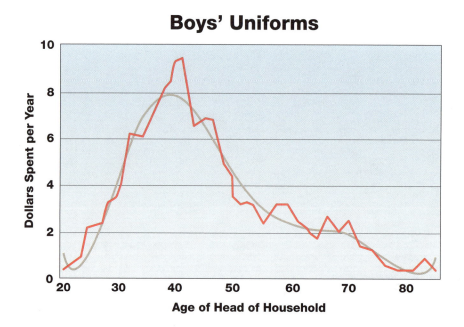

Figure 9.32

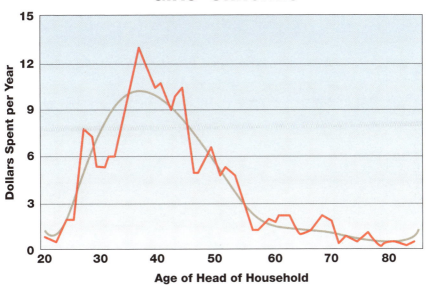

Figure 9.33

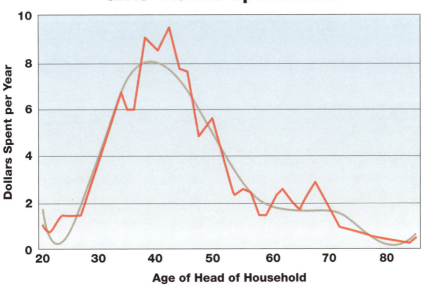

Figure 9.34

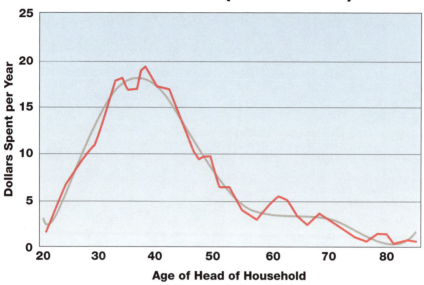

Figure 9.35

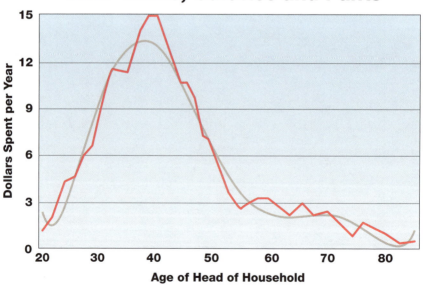

Figure 9.36

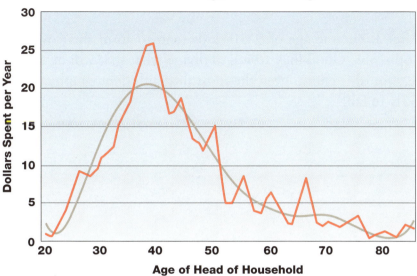

Figure 9.37

The nice aspect about infants is that you know what comes next. Today's infant is a toddler two years later and a kindergartener five years later.

Figures 9.15 through 9.37 all tell very similar stories. Spending on virtually all clothing and accessories for boys and girls peak in the late 30s or very early 40s. After this point, the lines get a little blurred. You may technically be buying adult clothes for the teenage kids by the government's definitions, and these purchases would happen in your 40s, not your 30s. So, true peak spending on the clothes of your children will generally be much later than these figures suggest. Take these particular charts with a healthy grain of salt.

The key to take away here is this: Once the new baby boom gets underway, you will have plenty of advanced notice to put a plan in place for profiting from the next stage of childhood development. Build a loyal client base among the mothers (and grandmothers) of infants, and they will be your customers for the next 8–10 years. Your business can mature along with their kids.

After about the age of 9–10, kids tend to form their own fashion opinions. Good luck trying to divine what that will be ahead of time… on this count, even the most in-depth demographic analysis is likely to fail!

Clothing and Accessories for Adults

Clothing and Accessories for Adults

Demographic trends point to a bright future for infant and children's clothing and accessories, even if a little patience is needed. The real boom is coming; we may just have to wait a few years.

I would love to tell you that I have good news for clothing and accessories for men and women, but that is not at all the case. The dominant buyers are consumers in their late 40s and early 50s, meaning that retreating Baby Boomers will be a major headwind for years to come. When you combine this with a lackluster economic backdrop, it is a recipe for very hard times at America's shopping malls. I expect to see major consolidation in the years ahead.

Marginal department stores like JC Penney and Sears probably will not survive, at least not in their current form and not without major new investment. This will create opportunities for the stronger competitors left behind, but it is still likely to be a rough several years in the meantime.

Smaller specialty shops will have a hard time as well. Just as a rising tide lifts all boats, it is when the tide goes out that you can see who has been swimming naked, to take a colorful quote from Warren Buffett. As the Boomers approached their peak spending years, there was enough money to go around. Even marginal stores with mediocre product lines could limp along indefinitely in that kind of macro environment. But with the Boomers retrenching and without a large, wealthy generation immediately coming up behind them, these are precisely the kinds of retail stores that fail.

The retailers that survive and thrive in the years ahead will be those that appeal to the fastest-growing demographics, such as urban, educated young professionals. Financial discipline is also important. The next few years will not be a time for borrowing and expanding, but rather for consolidating what you have and keeping your powder dry for the next great opportunity.

For entrepreneurs in this area, as a general rule to operate by, you want to figure out what the Echo Boomers will be buying and then get in front of them by a few years. They will not reach their peak spending years for another 25–30 years, but they are your next big market. With that said, let's jump into some specific products.

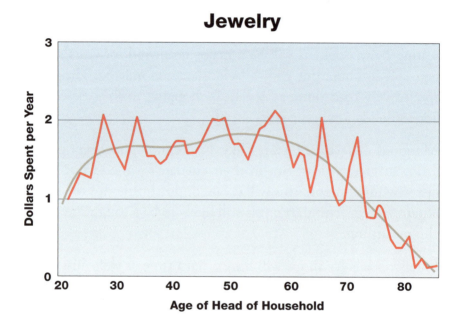

Figure 10.1

Jewelry is one area where spending is more constant over most of the family and adult cycle. (Figure 10.1). Spending peaks around the age of 57 and remains relatively strong for another decade, meaning that the Baby Boomers still have a little spending left in them, even if it is less extravagant than in years past. And there should also be strong spending by the Echo Boomers coming along and getting married increasingly into 2017, then demand should slow for several years until 2024 and then grow again until 2034–2035.

There is a large surge of jewelry buying in the mid-20s. Any ideas as to what that might be? Engagement rings, of course. An engagement ring and wedding bands is the first significant piece of jewelry that most men ever buy, though it certainly isn't their last.

I should stop here to make an important clarification that applies to quite a few products. Echo Boomer spending will generally not replace Baby Boomer spending. But in this chapter, we have to look for silver linings where we can find them, and wedding jewelry will be one of the few areas of growth for jewelers in an industry otherwise looking at tepid demand.

If your business concerns jewelry, prepare to make changes. You core customers, the Baby Boomers, are starting to peak. Grabbing a larger share of Echo Boomer engagement and wedding business is your best bet here.

Watches (Figure 10.2) are an interesting story. Spending peaks around the age of 59, when that Rolex you've always wanted finally becomes affordable. But it quickly falls from that point on. The Boomers still have a few years left here, but this window closes at the end of this decade.

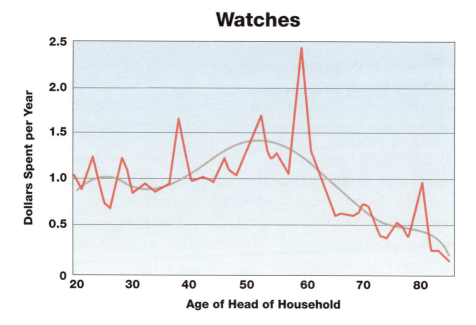

Figure 10.2

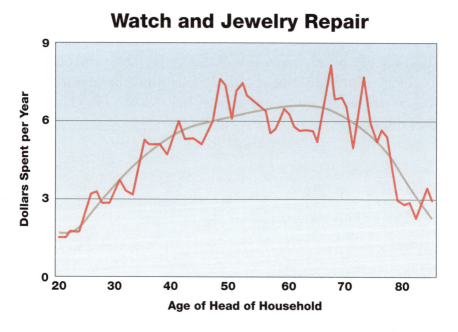

Figure 10.3

There should be opportunities for watch and jewelry repair (Figure 10.3). Americans spend more on repairing their watches and jewelry well into their 60s. Spending here peaks at age 67 and falls precipitously by the mid-70s.

If you own a watch or jewelry store, offering a new maintenance and repair service could be a viable growth business for you and might help you to partially offset lukewarm product sales. Again, in this environment, we take what we can get.

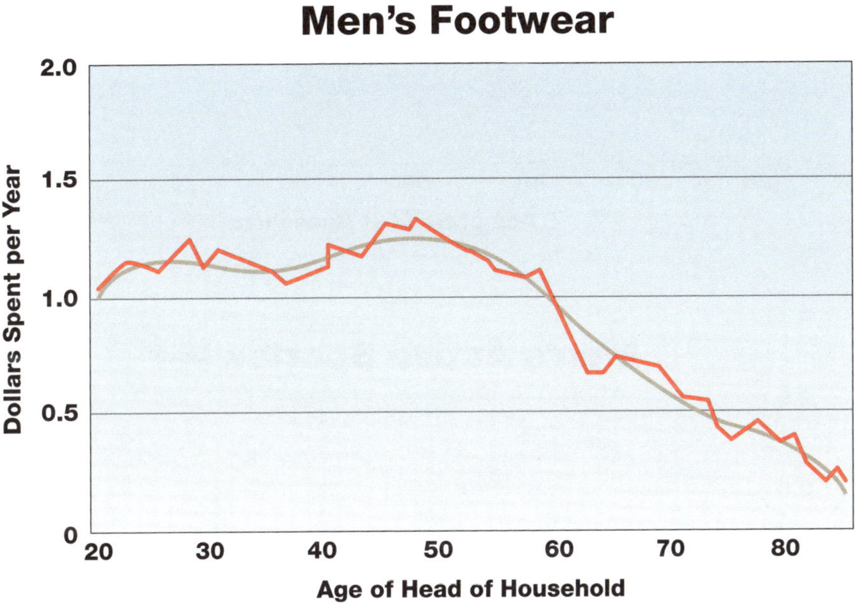

Men's Footwear

Figure 10.4

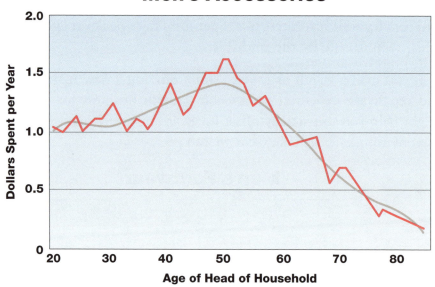

Figure 10.5

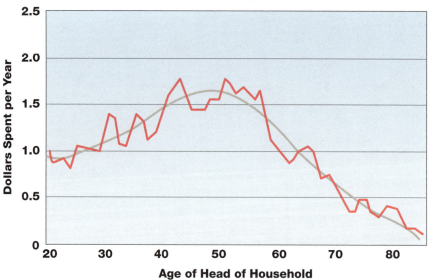

Figure 10.6

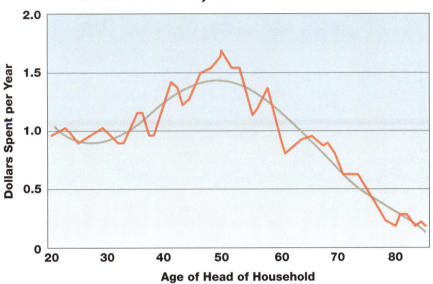

Figure 10.7

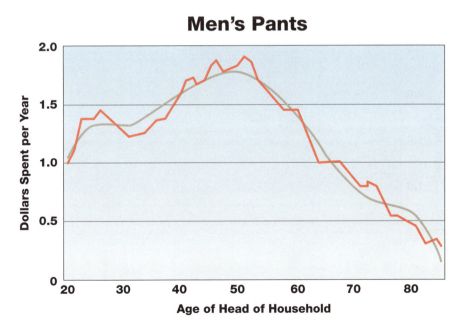

Figure 10.8

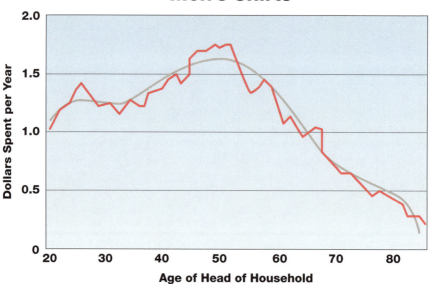

Figure 10.9

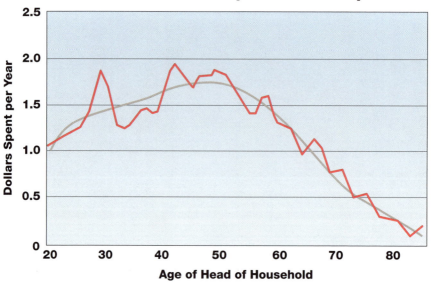

Figure 10.10

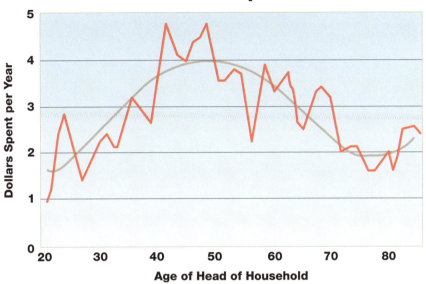

Figure 10.11

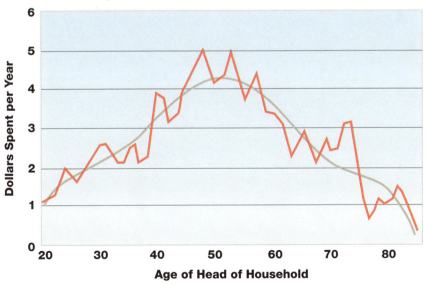

Figure 10.12

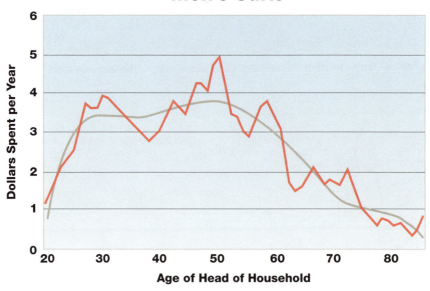

Figure 10.13

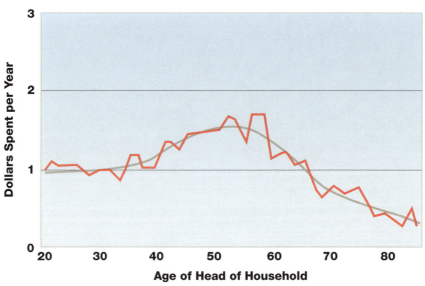

Figure 10.14

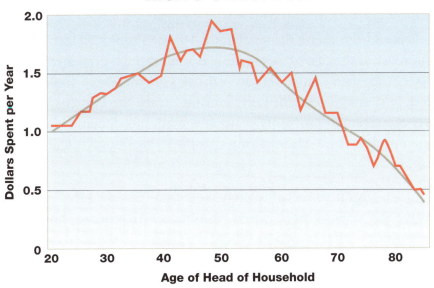

Figure 10.15

With products sold specifically for men, the outlook is unambiguously bad. The demographic demand curves for Figures 10.4 through 10.15 are almost identical. Demand starts low in the 20s, peaks in the late 40s or early 50s in line with peak overall spending, and then falls off a cliff.

There are a few exceptions worth noting. Men's footwear (Figure 10.4) remains relatively constant from the age of 20 to the age of 50 with a peak at age 49. The retrenchment of the Baby Boomers will still be felt, of course, and they are the largest generation and the biggest spenders. But at least compared with the rest of the products in this section, shoe sellers can expect sales to Echo Boomers to pick up a lot of the slack. This is not a growth market by any stretch, and I don't want you to get the wrong idea. It's just a product area that is "less bad" than the rest.

A 20-year old buys different shoes than a 50-year old. So, the stores that do well here will be the ones that successfully make the transition from a middle-aged clientele to a young clientele.

Demand for men's shorts (Figure 10.10) should be less dreadful than most of the rest of this section as well, though certainly far from good. And men's suits (Figure 10.13) comparatively looks pretty good, as demand remains fairly constant from the late 20s until the early 50s. Demand for suits peaks at age 50, but demand also has an earlier peak around 31, implying that the Echo Boomers will soon be "suiting up."

Again, I want to be completely clear that "less dreadful" does not mean good. Menswear in general is in for a rough decade ahead, and every product in this section should see lackluster demand due to demographic trends. But certain areas will be hit less hard than others.

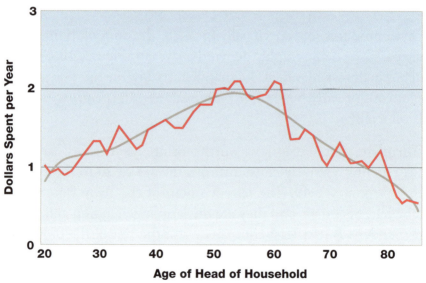

Figure 10.16

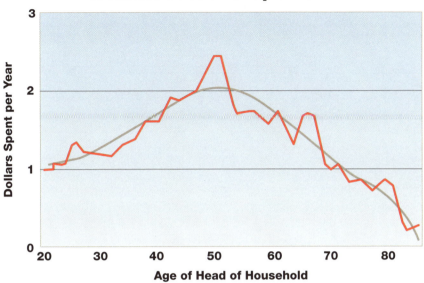

Figure 10.17

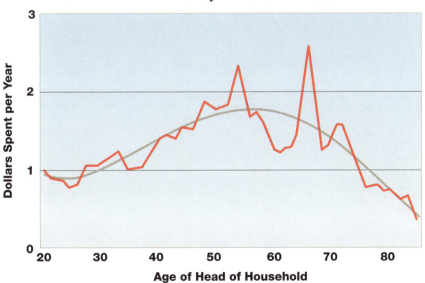

Figure 10.18

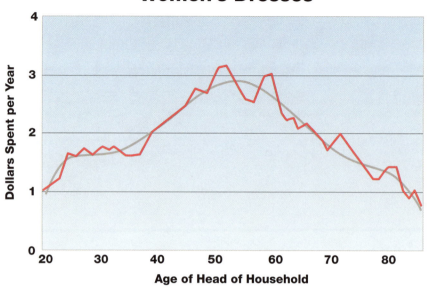

Figure 10.19

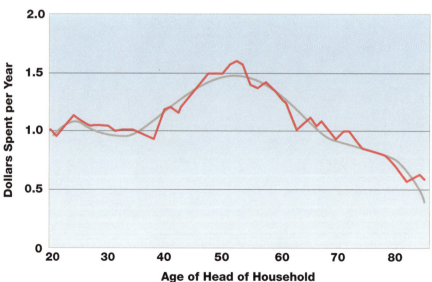

Figure 10.20

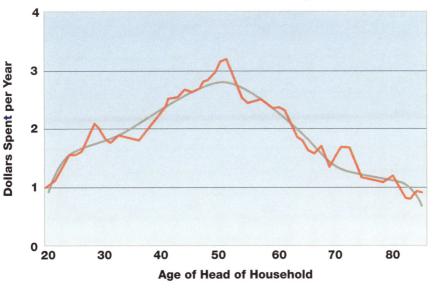

Figure 10.21

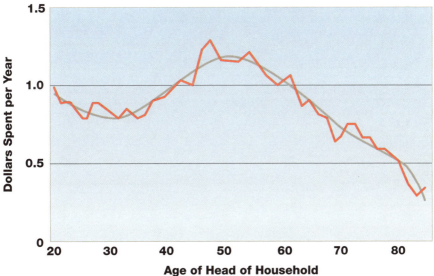

Figure 10.22

199

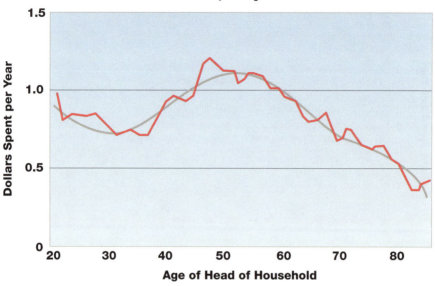

Figure 10.23

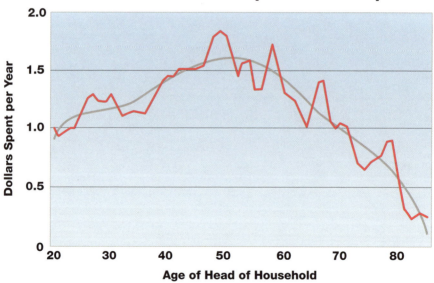

Figure 10.24

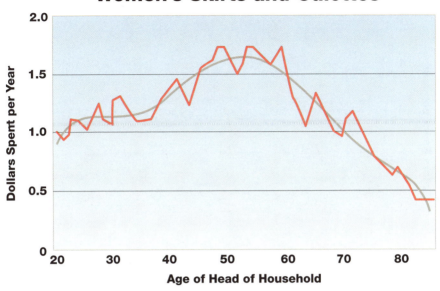

Figure 10.25

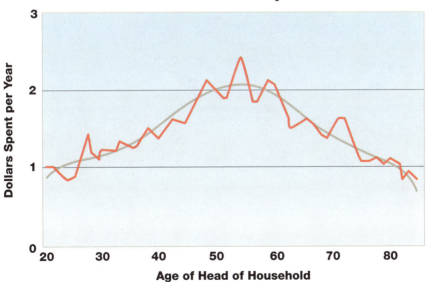

Figure 10.26

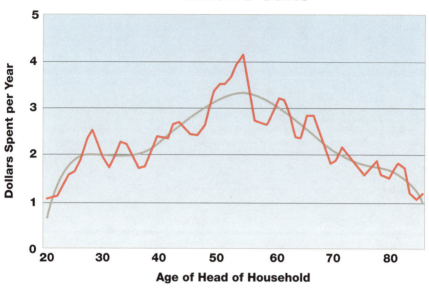

Figure 10.27

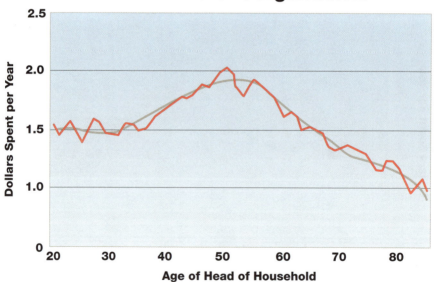

Figure 10.28

Figure 10.29

As a general rule, spending on women's clothing and accessories peaks slightly later than on those for men, but it is not enough to make a difference in our demographic forecast. Men's products peak in the very late 40s and early 50s; for women's products it is generally the early to mid-50s. But as Baby Boomer women are already at this stage of their lives, it's too late in the game for this information to be useful for a retailer.

And there is even less differentiation among women's products than men's. Women's pants (Figure 10.22) and blouses (Figure 10.23) have demand curves that are slightly less steep than, say, women's hosiery (Figure 10.21). But in virtually every case, spending has declined by the early to mid-50s.

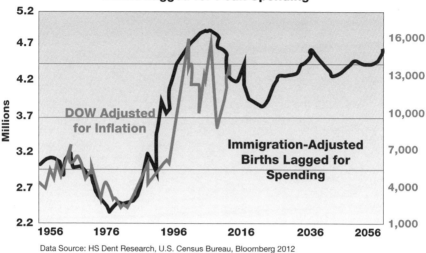

Figure 10.30

What are the key points to take away from this chapter? The clothing and accessories markets for men and women are completely dominated by consumers in their late 40s and early 50s. This was fantastic news when the Baby Boomers were entering this stage of their lives. But now that they have passed it, it is a nightmare scenario for retailers.

As a basic rule of thumb, you can use the Spending Wave (Figure 10.30) to estimate demand for men's and women's retail, as peak spending on these items is nearly identical to overall peak spending. As you can see here, the Spending Wave doesn't bottom out until 2020 and doesn't see another peak until the mid-2030s.

So, unless your specialty is selling to the late 20s or early 30s demographics (i.e., today's Echo Boomers), clothing and accessories are terrible businesses to be in. If your career is in this industry, you might want to seriously consider a career change. If that is not possible for you, do what you can to keep your overhead low and keep your expenses cut to the bone. Your best chance for growth is to be the last man standing as your competitors close down.

This page intentionally left blank.

Computers and Electronics

Computers and Electronics

This chapter will be a little shorter than the preceding ones, as the Consumer Expenditure Survey had fewer products with usable data. Still, there is good information and good food for thought here in the fast-moving area of computer and electronic products.

I'll start with a service that seems almost quaint in today's world of ubiquitous smartphones: pay phones and paid telephones (Figure 11.1). I include this graph mostly to illustrate how much the world has changed. Pay phones have all but disappeared from the American landscape. We still see them in airports, but no one uses them. I mean that quite literally. Over the past five years, I might have seen one person using an airport payphone. And it actually caught my attention as something unusual.

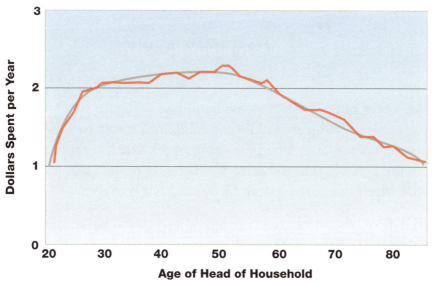

Figure 11.1

In product areas with fast technological change, demographics matter much less. It really doesn't matter that peak spending for pay phones happens around age 50. In the 1920s, it didn't matter that spending on horse buggy whips peaked at any particular age. When you've undergone a technological regime shift, the calculus changes.

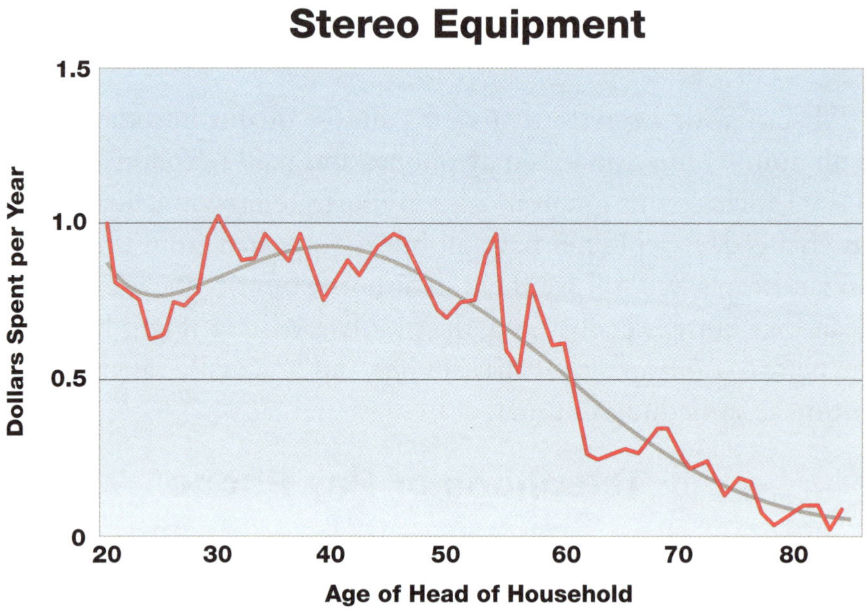

Stereo Equipment

Figure 11.2

Let's now take a look at stereo equipment (Figure 11.2), which is mostly a product for men. Like loud engines, young men love high-powered stereos. Spending peaks around 30, but it is fairly constant from the ages of 20 to the early 50s. By early middle age, a man can finally afford the stereo system he wanted as a teenager!

But here, the industry is changing and stereo equipment is becoming more of a niche market for true sound aficionados. The transition of music to mp3 and the popularity of products such as the iPod (and later smartphones) have moved music collections out of the living room and onto your computer's hard drive. And now, it's in the process of moving off of your hard drive and into the Internet cloud.

With all of this said, the Baby Boomers long ago passed the peak spending years for stereo equipment. Demographically, stereo equipment is attractive and will benefit from the rise of the Echo Boomers. But changing consumer tastes here are likely to be more important than demographic trends alone, so be careful. The best opportunities for an entrepreneur in this area might be in developing systems that tie together home media and allow universal control from a smartphone. Though be careful here because this could put you in direct competition with the likes of Apple and Google!

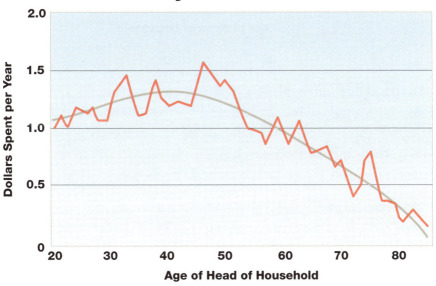

Figure 11.3

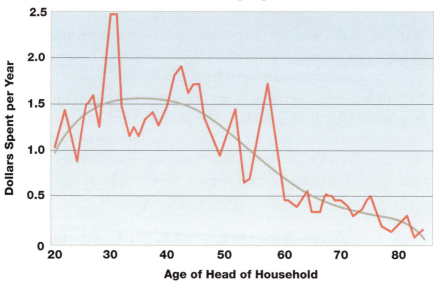

Figure 11.4

Demand for video players and camcorders (Figure 11.3) peaks at age 46 though it is relatively stable from 20 to 45. All else being equal, this is good from a demographic perspective. The damage from retreating Baby Boomers has already been done, so retailers can focus on the next big generation, the Echo Boomers.

However, all else is not equal, and this is another area where smartphones have become a major disruptor. Most medium-to-high-end phones now have a camcorder included in the hardware. It's nothing as sophisticated as a standalone camcorder from, say, Sony or Canon, but for many casual users it will be good enough for their purposes.

Sound equipment (Figure 11.4) is a little more immune from disruption from mobile phones, but this is also a relatively small niche market. There simply isn't a large mass market for PA systems, amplifiers, and the equipment that a garage band might need to put on a show.

Still, for what it is worth, this is a product area with excellent demographics. Spending peaks at age 30, making the 20-something Echo Boomers a prime market for growth.

This chapter offered little in the way of actionable business advice, but I hope you come away with a better appreciation for technological disruption. New technology is turning several old industries upside down. Electronics are the example used in this chapter, but books, newspapers, music and movies are all prime examples.

So, while I recommend you consider the demographic buying patterns of any industry before you invest, I cannot emphasize enough how important it is to also consider technological paradigm shifts as well. Even the most powerful demographic trends won't save a product that has been eclipsed by a new technology with mass acceptance. You don't want to be a maker of buggy whips in the age of the automobile!

This page intentionally left blank.

Entertainment and Travel

ENTERTAINMENT AND TRAVEL

The following chapter is something of a catch-all for travel and leisure activities. The prior chapters covered items that we buy in the course of our regular day-to-day affairs. This chapter covers products and services we buy when we want to, often for special occasions.

Consider cigars (Figure 12.1), perhaps the quintessential leisure product reserved for celebrations. In the popular mind, a cigar is a product for a discerning gentleman with good taste. The "ideal" customer might be the "Most Interesting Man in the World" from the Dos Equis beer commercials.

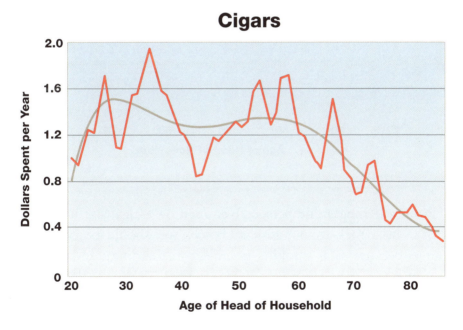

Figure 12.1

The data, however, paint a very different picture. Cigar and pipe tobacco product spending has a large initial peak at 26 followed by a larger peak at 34. It then drops significantly, though it has a brief comeback in the 50s. So much for stereotypes!

Compare this to demand for cigarettes (Figure 12.2), which more closely resembles the demand curve for broader peak spending. Demand peaks around the age of 38 but does not decline significantly until after 50.

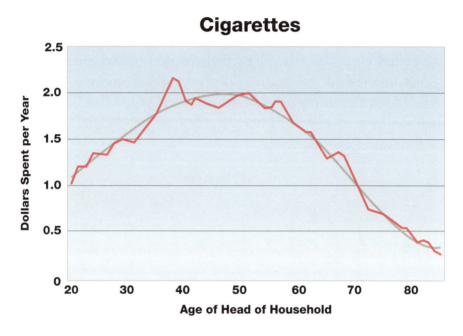

Figure 12.2

From a demographic perspective, opening a cigar bar would appear to be a rock solid business choice. You should be careful, of course, because cigar smoking is subject to trendiness and, particularly in larger cities, to pretty stringent restrictions on sales. Still, if you're not breaking any laws in doing so, selling cigars at your bar or restaurant might be a nice source of additional revenue.

Demographic trends are a lot less favorable for sports events tickets (Figure 12.3). Americans peak in their live sports spending around the age of 46, and it falls pretty aggressively after that. So, demographic trends suggest that professional sports franchises have a rough road in front of them. It might seem strange to say this at a time of record athlete salaries, but the demographics speak for themselves.

Technology also plays a role here. The quality of high definition home TVs has gotten to be so incredibly good, that watching a game at home on your couch is an attractive option.

What conclusions can we draw from this? Professional sports teams will depend more on TV and other revenues than on ticket sales in the years ahead. Will TV continue to pay as well as it has in the past? This will depend on the advertisers, of course, and I have no way of knowing this by looking at demographic statistics alone.

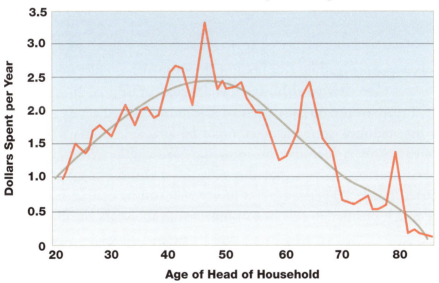

Figure 12.3

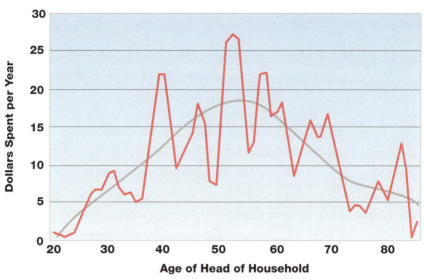

Figure 12.4

Few people reading this book will be sports franchise owners. But it is possible that your business is affected by sports. If you own a retail store or restaurant close to a stadium or if you act as a supplier to the stadiums your business might be affected. Similarly, stadium construction is lucrative business for construction companies and subcontractors. Given that the wave of stadium construction that started nearly 20 years ago has pretty well run its course, it's hard to see much positive in this line of business in the years ahead.

Life may get a little harder at boat marinas as well. Aside from a weak economy, which crimps sales of boats and other luxury items, demographic trends suggest that fees for docking and landing for boats and planes are in for a long decline (Figure 12.4). Demand peaks around the age of 52 and then goes into steep decline.

The same is true of admission fees to movies, theater, concerts and opera (Figure 12.5). Though demand is strong among Americans in their 20s and 30s, it significantly higher among those in the late 40s.

Overall spending peaks around the age of 50. Movies are the biggest component here, and the movie industry is already suffering due to rampant piracy and out-of-control costs; add to this a decline in the spending of their core demographic and you have a recipe for disaster.

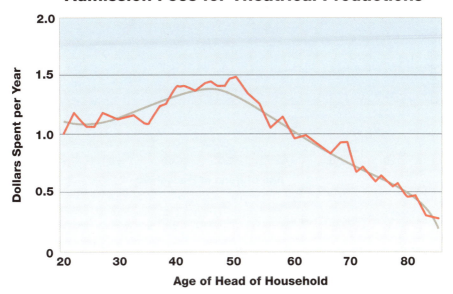

Figure 12.5

Life should be pretty good for America's bartenders for another few years. Sales of alcohol in restaurants, cafes, and bars (Figure 12.6) have two distinct sets of peaks, first at 22 and 30 and again at 54 and 60.

Any thoughts as to why?

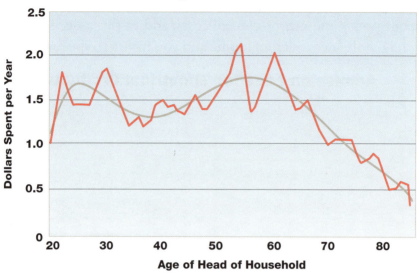

Figure 12.6

Try kids. Once your kids are born, you go out to eat less, and when you take your children with you, you are a lot less likely to order a drink. But as your children get older and eventually leave the nest, you have the luxury of enjoying a nice night out and the disposable income to buy a cocktail or two.

The next few years will be perhaps the best years for bar and restaurant owners in American history. Both the Baby Boomers and the Echo Boomers are in their prime "boozing it up" years. Unfortunately, it won't last. Both demographic groups will soon go into a long decline.

If you own a bar and contemplated selling, now might be a good time. Because starting next decade, demographic trends are going to take a serious turn for the worse.

Moving in to travel-related expenses, demographic trends are actually pretty good. Empty nester Baby Boomers will be a good source of revenue for the travel and leisure industry for quite some time.

Consider airlines (Figure 12.7). Airlines are a terrible business to be in. Warren Buffett once joked that the easiest way to become a millionaire is to start with a billion dollars and buy an airline. You have continuous problems with labor unrest, sensitivity to oil prices and to the overall health of the economy, and huge capital outlays that typically have to be paid for with debt. And these are during good times!

Demand for airline fares is strong through most of the 50s with two peaks around age 54 and age 60. The demographic trends for intercity (i.e. long distance) bus fares (Figure 12.8) and ship fares (Figure 12.9) are some of the best of any product or service discussed in this book.

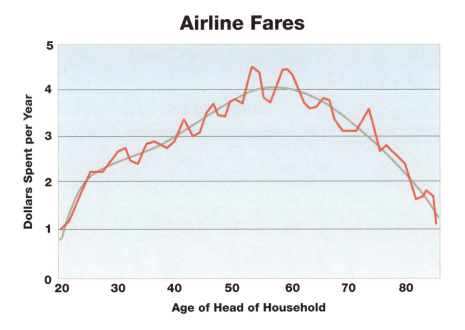

Figure 12.7

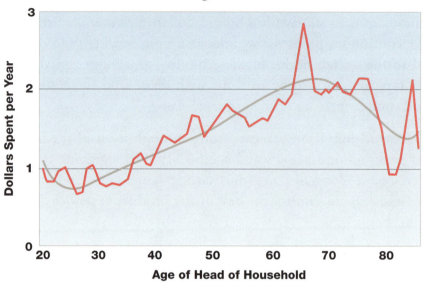

Figure 12.8

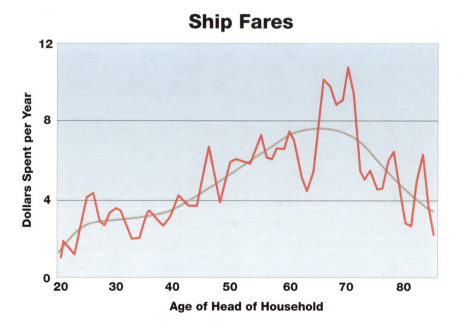

Figure 12.9

After older people realize that overseas travel is stressful and often difficult, they switch from airlines to cruise ships with no jet lag or hassles and where you can just get stuffed with food and booze. That industry is strongest from age 60 to age 70 before declining. Hence, overseas airline travel should do well into around 2021, albeit with headwinds from a difficult economy. Cruise ships should be strongest from 2022–2031.

You can't run out and buy an airline as a way to profit from this, but auxiliary businesses such as airport shuttles might be a viable option. How do you profit from these trends? That is a trickier question to answer. Travel agencies are in terminal decline due to cheaper Internet options, and in the online world you're competing against the likes of Priceline, Expedia, and other established players. The challenge for entrepreneurs will be to find ways to profit from these trends given the disruption that technology has wrought for the "old fashioned" travel industry.

Lodging away from home (Figure 12.10) peaks earlier than most travel-related expenses, around age 53. Hotel occupancy rates are also affected by business travel, which is in turn affected by the broader economy. So, in general, it is safe to say that lodging is an area in this broader industry that can be ignored.

Spending on entertainment expenses (Figure 12.11) and gasoline (Figure 12.12) on out-of-town trips both have late peak spending ages. Gasoline is one that can probably be ignored; I included it only to show the contrast between total gasoline purchases, which peaks in the late 40s (see Chapter 8) and gasoline purchased while traveling, which peaks more than a decade later.

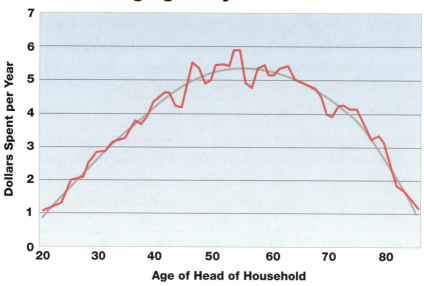

Figure 12.10

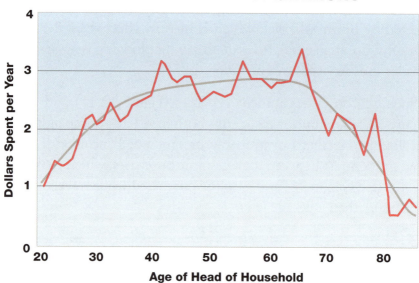

Figure 12.11

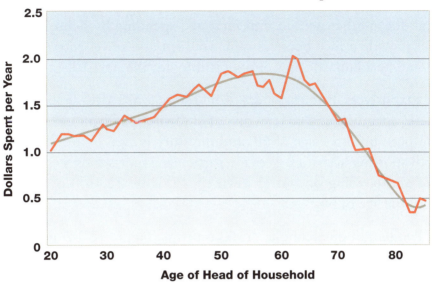

Figure 12.12

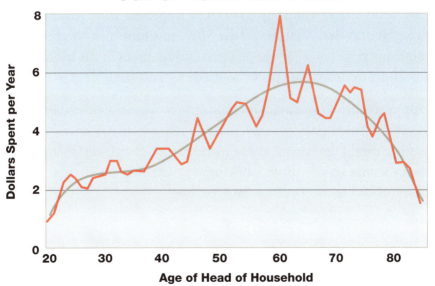

Figure 12.13

Entertainment expenses have excellent demographics in front of them. Peak spending is not until age 65, so the Baby Boomers won't peak for another decade, and increased spending by Echo Boomers will provide a nice boost as well. Tourism and travel entertainment should be a fantastic area of opportunity for the next 10–15 years.

Taxi drivers in tourist areas should have a nice decade in front of them. Spending on taxi fares on out of town trips (Figure 12.13) does not peak until the age of 60, and the story is even better for resorts with sporting activities. Fees for participant sports such as golf, tennis, and bowling on out of town trips (Figure 12.14) do not peak until the age of 66.

Food and non-alcoholic drinks on trips (Figure 12.15) peaks earlier, around 54, and auto rental on trips (Figure 12.16) peaks at 59.

Travel items, such as luggage (Figure 12.17) peaks at 50, making this a less attractive product segment.

"Travel and leisure" is a broad category, and spending on some items peaks earlier than others. But as a general rule, Americans are still active travelers well into their 50s and often into their 60s. And Americans who travel at those ages tend to spend a lot more money than 20-something backpackers or young families.

Opportunities here are almost limitless. There will be demand for everything from golf pros to massage therapists. A travel-oriented business might be an ideal "semi-retirement" project for a Boomer who wants to continue working and earning an income but for whom office life has become unappealing.

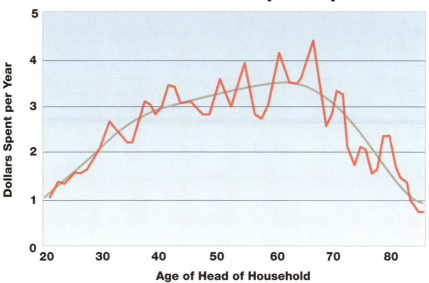

Figure 12.14

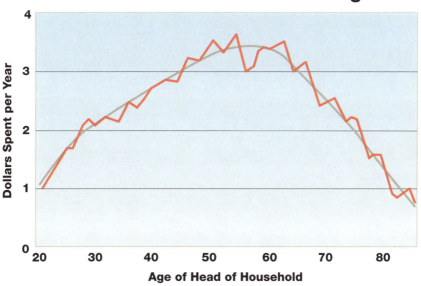

Figure 12.15

Figure 12.16

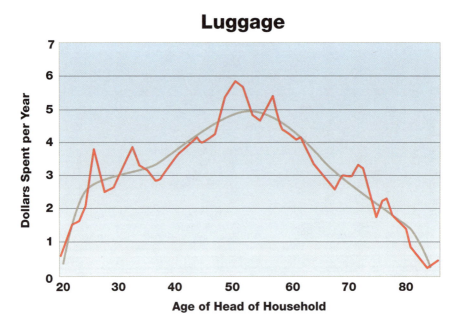

Figure 12.17

The Baby Boomers' Spending Wave has already crested, and from this point on they will progressively spend less money on virtually everything. But pleasure travel is a clear exception, and entrepreneurs can still profit from this trend, though time is of the essence here.

There is one final travel and leisure segment that is worth mentioning: RVs and campers.

For many Americans, the retirement dream is not a beach house or frequent cruises or resort stays, but rather the adventure of the open road. With the kids out of the house and with more time at their disposal, buying an RV gives them the opportunity to explore America at their own pace and allowing for a sense of "home" while on the road.

As you can see in Figure 12.18, RVs are purchased almost exclusively by Americans in their late 50s and early 60s with a peak at age 61 just before the average age of retirement at 63. You don't see too many college kids driving them, due in part to their high cost (fully loaded RVs can cost more than a house), though an RV might make for quite the spring break.

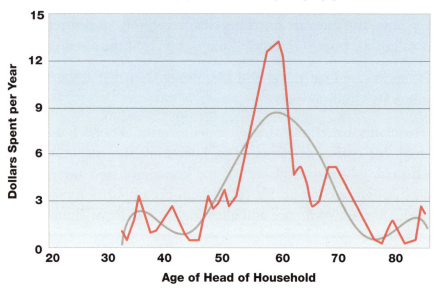

Figure 12.18

Health Care

Health Care

Whenever I mention the words "demographics" and "Baby Boomers" to a group of people, the first question I get asked is "What about health care?"

It's true; Baby Boomers are going to be using a lot more health care as they age. This has big implications for Americans since most health expenses are paid by insurance companies, to which we pay premiums, or by government programs like Medicare and Medicaid, to which we pay via taxes.

Health care is already an enormous chunk of the U.S. economy, coming in around 20%. It is almost mindboggling that health care consumes so much of our economy given that, until now, we have had a relatively young country without a lot of medical needs. Our health spending as a percentage of GDP is roughly double the size of every other industrialized country. This points to a very flawed system in which medical professionals are incentivized to practice their trade in a costly, inefficient manner.

Please don't think this is a criticism of doctors or an allegation of greed. Doctors actually made far less than they did in the 1980s and 1990s when you adjust for inflation. Yes, you read that right. Even as medical costs have exploded, doctors are getting paid less. This is a bad system for everyone involved.

I expect major changes in the health care industry in the years ahead, which will probably be controversial to many readers. Keep in mind, I am not necessarily advocating any of these policies, I am merely telling you what I think will happen.

The biggest will be medical rationing. The most controversial aspects of the Obamacare legislation was the allegation that government "death panels" would decide which patients live and which patients die. This was unsettling to many because we like to think that these kinds of decisions should be made with our families and our doctors, not cold, impersonal government bureaucrats.

But if you frame the question differently, Americans might have a very different view. "Do you think that the government should avoid wasting Medicare money on unnecessary procedures that are unlikely to improve the health of the patient?"

Suddenly, rationing doesn't seem quite so bad when presented like this. Again, I'm not defending Obamacare or expressing any opinion at all on the program. I'm just making a point that change is needed if we are to keep the medical system solvent, and the change is going to be controversial.

Through Medicare, the government pays more in doctor and hospital bills during the last two months of patients' lives than it does for the Department of Homeland Security or the Department of Education. That's not total spending; it's just the spending on those patients in the final two months before death. And 20 to 30% of these medical expenses have no meaningful impact in that they are "tests" and procedures being performed on terminally ill patients.[18]

Chronically ill people in the last two years of their lives account for 32% of total Medicare spending. Breaking it down further, Medicare pays for one-third of the cost of treating cancer in the final year of life, and 78% of that spending occurs in the last month.[19]

Doctors are programmed to do everything they can to prolong a patient's life, no matter what the probability of success. At some point, you have to assign a dollar value to the cost of prolonging a life by that extra six months or so. Medical resources are not inexhaustible, and it is better to spend them on patients with longer life expectancies. And frankly, if presented honest odds, many Americans might prefer to simply treat the pain symptoms and accept death on their own terms rather than risk dying on the operating table in a procedure that most likely won't work.

Personally, I don't like the idea of having my health care rationed. I prefer to be given honest assessments of the odds of success and honest assessments of the costs so that I can make my own decision. But frankly, I don't see that happening, so we're left with some sort of rationing.

Without rationing of services, the only alternative is the rationing of the market, and by this I mean the de facto rationing that comes with higher prices. When prices rise, we can afford less.

At any rate, this debate will rage for years, and I do not expect that either party will be honest with American voters about the choices we face as a country. The Democrats prefer to make the choices for you, and the Republicans prefer to live in a fantasy world in which choices don't have to be made.

This is a long way of saying that demographics are not the only trend you need to watch here. Changes in government policies can have a major impact on the prices charged for medical services and on your ability to get reimbursed for them. And change is coming. I can't tell you what precise form it will take, because this will depend on negotiations between the president and Congress. But change will come, and you have to be ready for anything.

With all of this said, let's dig into the demographic trends of medicine, starting with physician services that peak around age 58 (Figure 13.1), hospital services around age 60 (Figure 13.2) and dental services around age 45 (Figure 13.3). Doctors and hospitals will do well into the end of this decade as such expenditures are more recession-resistant.

It is somewhat shocking that spending on regular physician services peaks in the late 50s, and it cannot be explained by Medicare picking up the tab. Medicare does not kick in until several years later.

Likewise, hospital services, such as operating, recovery, ICU, and x-rays have demographic spending patterns that will surprise many. There is a huge surge into the early 30s, which corresponds to child birth. After a small lull, spending increases again until age 60 before falling significantly. The best explanation here is that, as we age beyond our 50s, we tend to do fewer things that would get us hospitalized, such as blowing out a knee playing tennis or skiing.

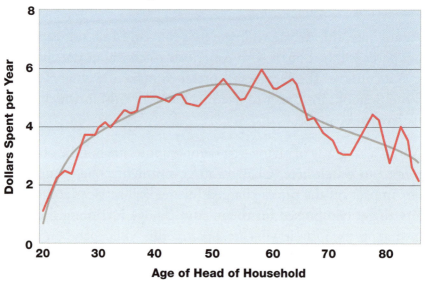

Figure 13.1

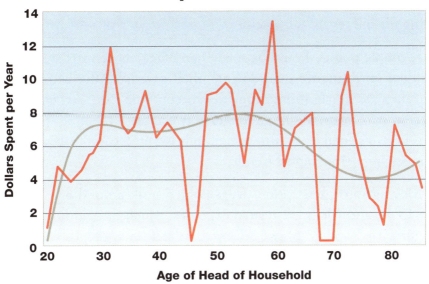

Figure 13.2

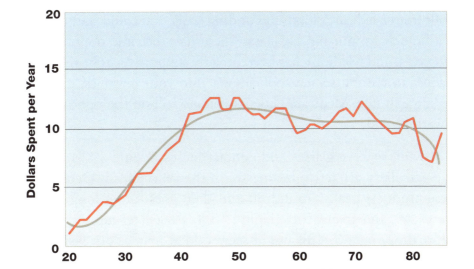

Figure 13.3

Dental services peak much earlier, around the age of 45, but they never really drop off much. Our teeth continue to need cleaning and fixing for the rest of our lives.

A couple points should be made here. First, as dentists are less dependent on insurance than doctors, their practices offer better stability. They are not immune from macroeconomic risk—when money is tight, Americans might go longer between teeth cleanings or forego non-urgent dental work. But overall, this is a profession that is resilient to changing demographic trends.

Moving into prescription drugs, which peak around age 77 (Figure 13.4), and Medicare-related expenses, which peak around age 74 (Figures 13.5 and 13.6), we see exactly the kind of graphs you would expect to see. Prescription drug expenses rise from young adulthood to death. Medicare-related expenses kick in later, once we qualify for Medicare, but then they rise for the rest of our lives.

Profiting from these trends is tricky. You could invest in a pharmacy, of course, but there is already a lot of competition on that front. To profit from Medicare's looming funding crisis, you could start or invest in a home care nursing business. These have become popular in recent years, and Medicare has been broadly supportive. Your risk is that changes to reimbursement policies cut into your revenues, but given the surge in new Medicare patients you are still on the right side of a powerful trend.

Moving on, eye glasses and contact lenses (Figure 13.7) will not be particularly attractive businesses in the years ahead. Demand for these products peaks around 50 and then goes into a long decline. Eye exams and treatments (Figure 13.8) peak later around age 60, before dropping off. This might seem odd at first, as our vision does not get better after the age of 60. Still, older consumers go longer in between new pairs of glasses and are less likely to use contacts.

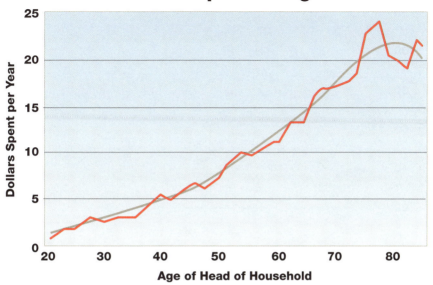

Figure 13.4

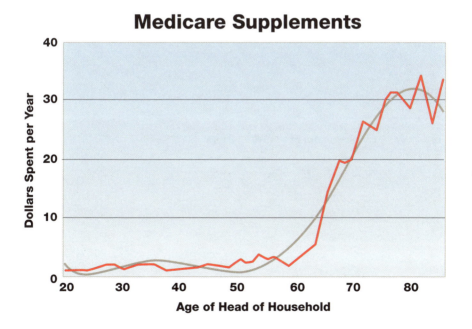

Figure 13.5

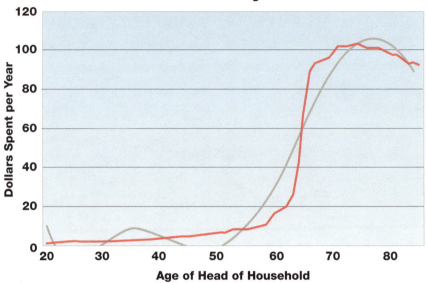

Figure 13.6

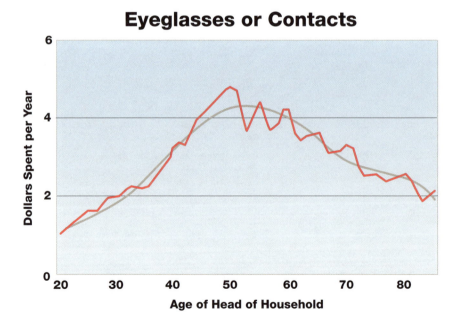

Figure 13.7

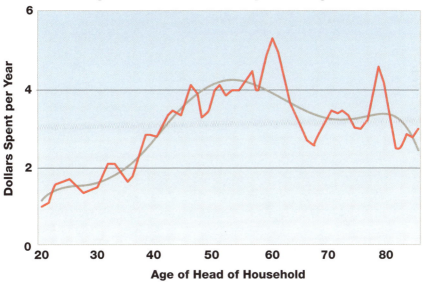

Figure 13.8

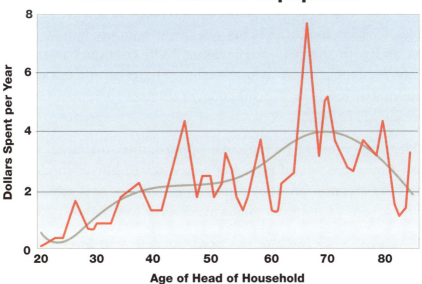

Figure 13.9

237

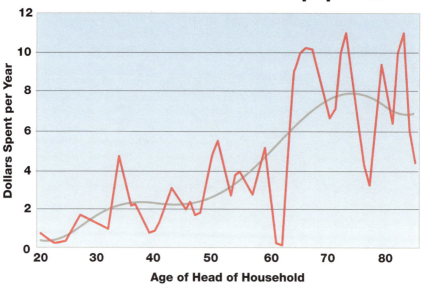

Figure 13.10

Demand for certain medical products peaks much later than you might have expected. For example, purchases of thermometers, syringes, ice bags and other items you might associate more with children and with sports injuries (Figure 13.9) continues to rise until nearly 70. Purchases of "convalescent" equipment such as crutches, wheelchairs, braces and Ace bandages (Figure 13.10) actually peak after the age of 70.

Here, there might be potential opportunities for rental services. Most Americans would probably prefer not to buy a wheelchair or crutches for conditions they expect to be temporary. A rental service for these sorts of products might make sense in your area.

And finally, we come to the products that tend to be purchased most by older Americans, such as hearing aids (Figure 13.11), and convalescent care in a nursing home (Figure 13.12). Demand for each of these continues to rise until the end of the graph.

Again, while the demographic trends here are obvious and powerful, profiting from them might be somewhat tricky. There are not a lot of opportunities to sell hearing aids, for example. Nursing home investment might be a viable option, though if you lack nurses' training it might be best to invest as a passive investor in an existing project.

Overall, the best opportunities in medicine in the next decade will be in finding ways to cut costs without reducing the quality of care. This is easier said than done, and I have no easy or obvious answers for you. The problem is there. It's up to you to find the solution.

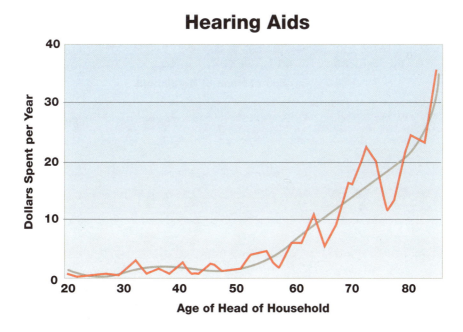

Figure 13.11

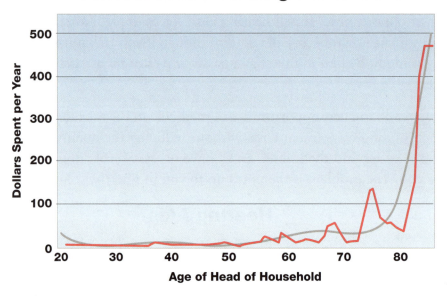

Figure 13.12

Professional Services

Professional Services

In this last chapter, we are going to cover professional services, which covers a broad array of services that could loosely be described as financial, legal and other white collar professional services. These sorts of services tend to be paid by higher income Americans, but nearly everyone pays them in some form or another.

I'll start with accounting fees (Figure 14.1) and legal fees (Figure 14.2), which in this case does not include real estate closing costs.

Accounting fees have an initial peak around the age of 61, decline for nearly two decades, and then rise strongly until a final peak from 79 to 81. Some of the late surge is no doubt due to estate planning and tax planning, both of which are excellent growth practices right now.

Interestingly, legal fees peak fairly early, around 37, but have several subsequent peaks into the 80s. Few Americans need the services of a criminal defense attorney; most of the legal fees paid by Americans are for marriage, divorce, and family issues and later in life for estate planning issues. Unfortunately, I cannot recommend law as a career path right now, as there is an enormous glut of lawyers. There are twice as many law school graduates as there are legal jobs,[20] which means that legal wages have nowhere to go but down in most practice areas.

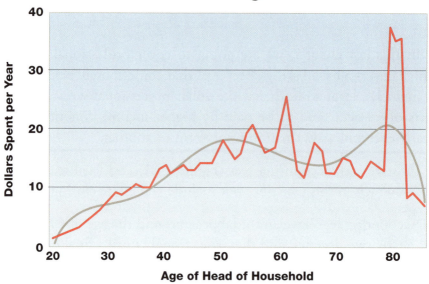

Figure 14.1

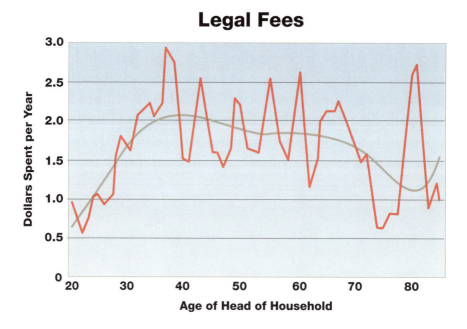

Figure 14.2

Charges for checking accounts (Figure 14.3) and other banking services peak fairly early, around the age of 51, and decline steeply thereafter. Yet demand for safe deposit box rentals (Figure 14.4) continues to rise until very late in life. It's hard to gauge the business opportunities here, as the primary providers of these services are banks. But the demographic trends are quite clear.

Computer information services (Figure 14.5) is different than other professional services in that it is more technical. And demographic trends here are not positive. Spending has a double peak at 46 and 50, meaning that the Baby Boomers will be spending less on these services.

As older Americans use computers, tablets, and smartphones more, there will be new opportunities to serve an older demographic than has ever been served before. If this graph were to be redrawn five years from now, I would expect the after-50 drop-off to be much less steep. But the key insight of this graph is that demand for traditional computer information services will wane in the years ahead.

Finally, we get to two services we would rather not think about — the purchase and upkeep of cemetery lots (Figure 14.6) and funeral, burial or cremation expenses (Figure 14.7). Americans don't like to think about death, but they do often plan ahead. Cemetery lot buying has an early peak at 66 and again at 73 before rising a final time in the 80s. Funeral expenses peak around age 78, the average life expectancy today. That will continue to increase at least one year every decade.

Figure 14.3

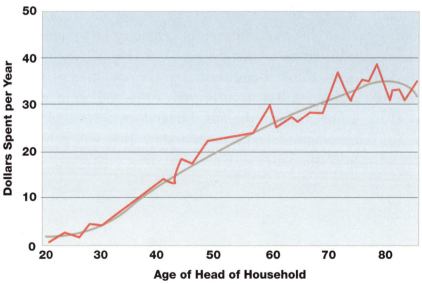

Figure 14.4

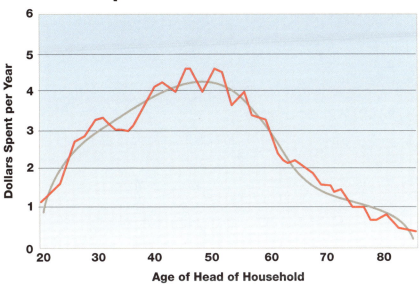

Figure 14.5

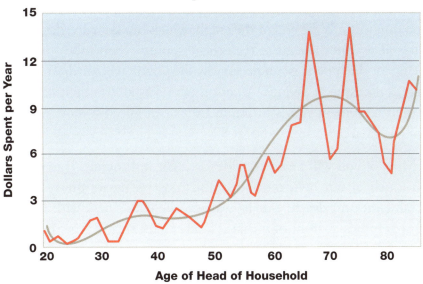

Figure 14.6

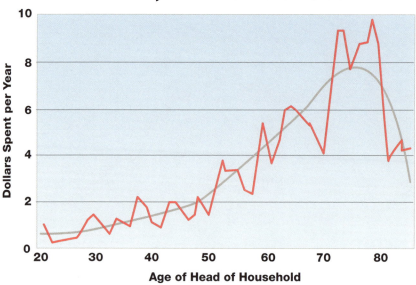

Figure 14.7

I know the question on your mind: How do funeral expenses decline after the late 70s? There are three issues at work here. First, the data gets a little thin towards the end of the graph, which can skew the data slightly at the edges. But there is also the issue of spouses. Remember, the person paying for the funeral is not necessarily the person who died. And finally, there is the issue of savings. A person who dies at 70 might have more of their retirement funds intact and thus can afford a more expensive funeral that a person who dies at 80.

Most of you will never consider a career in funerals. It reminds us too much of our own mortality, and most of us are pretty uncomfortable around death. But it is an excellent business with excellent demographics in front of it that is likely to see steady growth up until 2040.

I'm not recommending that you go to mortuary school. Most funeral homes are family owned and operated, and those are not the kinds of jobs you can just walk into. But I would recommend making an investment in an existing home or partnering with existing owner operators who might need capital for expansion or who might have run into financial problems for unrelated reasons.

There will be a boom in final expenses, but you have plenty of time here. Remember, the largest cohort of the Baby Boomers are only 52 right now. Given current life expectancy, they might have another 40–50 years of life left. In the meantime, demand might actually be a little slack. Births went into a sharp decline from 1924 to 1933 before turning up. These people are 80 to 89 today.

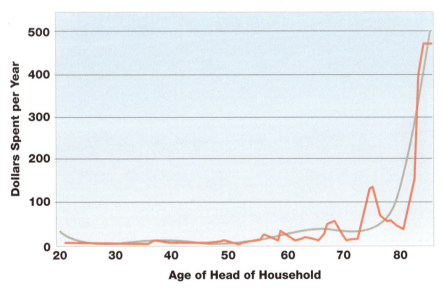

Figure 14.8

Perhaps the best opportunities for real estate development will come from nursing homes and assisted living facilities (Figure 14.8), which peaks around age 81–84. Such facilities typically seem to be in short supply and the Baby Boom has not even entered this cycle yet. This arena should explode from around 2018 into at least 2042.

So, there will come a time to position yourself to profit from the final expenses of America's largest and richest generation, but I would not recommend any investments until the end of this decade.

Conclusion

In the introduction, I laid out my case that the United States is facing a prolonged period of sluggish growth due to the aging of the Baby Boomers beyond their peak spending years and due to the unwinding of the greatest debt bubble in history. Overall, our economy faces very difficult challenges ahead. And other than my comments in Chapter 13, I barely even touched on the fiscal issues facing our government.

Our national debt is growing by more than a trillion dollars per year at a time of no inflation. And as if that wasn't bad enough news, it gets so much worse. Social Security and Medicare, which are designed to be funded by their own distinct tax streams, aren't even part of the current funding problem… yet. Social Security's expenditures for current retirees started to exceed income from current workers in 2010. This means that the federal government had to make up the difference through its general fund to the tune of $49 billion in 2010 and $45 billion in 2011. While $49 billion sounds like a lot of money to you or me, it is a drop in the bucket in a $3.5 trillion federal budget. The real deficits will come in the early 2020s when the Baby Boomers born in the late 1950s and early 1960s start to collect their payments.

For Medicare, the story is even worse. Congress has already had to dip deeply into the general fund to pay for current expenses. Barring major cost clampdowns, which will be unpopular with retired Baby Boomer voters, these expenses will absolutely explode in the 2020s as the Boomers enter the high-health-care-consuming stage of their lives.

This is the point I want to drive home: Our government is running record deficits at a time of relative peace and at a time when Social

Security and Medicare costs are still not a major burden. This is the calm before the storm, when we should be building up surpluses to tide us over in the difficult period to come. Instead, we're running deficits that should be shocking and appalling to all Americans. Can you imagine how bad it's going to get in the next decade?

I'm not being defeatist when I say that these debts will never be paid back. They won't be. It's the honest truth, and anyone who says to the contrary is either delusional or a charlatan. The only way they can be "paid back" would be through debt monetization by the Federal Reserve, in which the Fed essentially "forgave" the outstanding amounts on the bonds it holds. But this brings with it a whole new set of problems, such as potential currency collapse.

Is your head spinning yet?

In the years ahead, we will face a host of overlapping crises that will make life very difficult for American business professionals. The reduction in spending by the Baby Boomers and the process of deleveraging in the financial sector can be thought of as a balloon that is deflating. Other factors in the economy will determine how fast it deflates, but they cannot plug the leak. The air is seeping out, and there is nothing we can do about it!

Government policy adds another wrinkle to this scenario. How will our government respond to the challenges I outline? Will they cut spending and pull more dollars out of the economy? Or will they delay reform for another few years and risk creating an even bigger crisis later?

There is no way to answer this, and it doesn't make sense to spend our time calculating scenarios that in the end will depend on the whims of politicians. Instead, we can focus on demographic trends, which are highly predictable. Even in a terrible economy marked by slow growth and governmental uncertainty, there will be excellent opportunities for forward-thinking entrepreneurs and investors. I hope the demographic analysis we performed in this book will give you a framework for seeking out those opportunities.

Best wishes in the years ahead,

—Harry S. Dent, Jr.

This page intentionally left blank.

End Notes

1. The "demography is destiny" quote is attributed to the French philosopher Auguste Comte. "Demographics are the future that has already been written" is attributed to demographer and writer Philip Longman.

2. "Elderly at Record Spurs Japanese Stores," Bloomberg, May 9, 2012 http://www.bloomberg.com/news/2012-05-09/elderly-at-record-spurs-japan-stores-chase-1-4-trillion.html

3. Taylor, Alex. "Harley Davidson's Aging Biker Problem." *Fortune*, September 17, 2010

4. Taha, Nadia. "The Cost, in Dollars, of Raising a Child," *The New York Times*, November 13, 2012 http://bucks.blogs.nytimes.com/2012/11/13/the-cost-in-dollars-of-raising-a-child/

5. U.S. Bureau of Labor Statistics Consumer Expenditure Survey site: http://www.bls.gov/cex/ For any philosophy buffs out there, this is a variant of the Fallacy of Composition concept in what is good for the individual is bad for the group and vice versa.

6. Levin, Adam. "Is College Tuition the Next Bubble," ABC News, March 24, 2012. http://abcnews.go.com/Business/bubble-time-cap-college-tuition/story?id=15987539

7. Ellis, Blake. "Average Student Loan Debt Nears $27,000," CNNMoney, October 18, 2012 http://money.cnn.com/2012/10/18/pf/college/student-loan-debt/index.html

8. Jamrisko, Michelle. "Cost of College Degree in U.S. Soars 12 Fold," *Bloomberg*, August 15, 2012 http://www.bloomberg.com/news/2012-08-15/cost-of-college-degree-in-u-s-soars-12-fold-chart-of-the-day.html

9. U.S. Bureau of Labor Statistics, January 28, 2013 http://www.bls.gov/emp/ep_chart_001.htm

10. Lewin, Tamar. "Record Number Complete High School and College," *The New York Times*, November 5, 2012. http://www.nytimes.com/2012/11/06/education/record-numbers-of-young-americans-earn-bachelors-degree.html?_r=0

11. "Births: Preliminary Data for 2011." The Centers for Disease Control, October 3, 2012 http://www.cdc.gov/nchs/data/nvsr/nvsr61/nvsr61_05.pdf

12. Gottfried, Miriam. "Sex or Sleep," *Barron's*, May 14, 2012. http://online.barrons.com/article/SB50001424053111903623804577384290642721710.html

13. U.S. Bureau of Economic Analysis http://www.bea.gov/newsreleases/national/gdp/2013/pdf/gdp4q12_adv.pdf

14. U.S. Auto Sales: http://ycharts.com/indicators/auto_sales

15. Hargreaves, Steve. "Young Americans Ditch the Car," CNNMoney, September 17, 2012 http://money.cnn.com/2012/09/17/news/economy/young-buying-cars/index.html

16. Lowry, Joan. "Young Americans Less Likely to Drive" *BusinessWeek*, April 5, 2012 http://www.businessweek.com/ap/2012-04/D9TV0JJG2.htm

17. Court, Andy. "The Cost of Dying," CBS News, August 6, 2010. http://www.cbsnews.com/8301-18560_162-6747002.html

18. "Facing Death," PBS.org, http://www.pbs.org/wgbh/pages/frontline/facing-death/facts-and-figures/

19. Fletcher, Chris. "A Message to Aspiring Lawyers," *Wall Street Journal*, January 2, 2013 http://online.wsj.com/article/SB10001424127887323320404578213223967518096.html

20. Social Security and Medicare Trustees Report 2012 http://www.ssa.gov/oact/trsum/index.html